# best of
# Dick Martin
# CHRISTMAS

*Oh, the many joys of Christmas! Giving gifts, celebrating with family and friends, and don't forget those fun holiday projects! Whether you're a seasoned plastic canvas stitcher, or just getting started, you'll love these beautiful pieces by designer Dick Martin. Our fabulous Yuletide collection features projects you can make in a snap, as well as extravagant pieces worthy of the time spent to create them. From adorable tree ornaments to glittery tissue box covers, you're sure to find the perfect addition to your merry celebration.*

LEISURE ARTS, INC.
Little Rock, Arkansas

## EDITORIAL STAFF

**Vice President and Editor-at-Large:** Anne Van Wagner Childs
**Vice President and Editor-in-Chief:** Sandra Graham Case
**Director of Designer Relations:** Debra Nettles
**Special Projects Coordinator:** Jane Kenner Prather
**Editorial Director:** Susan Frantz Wiles
**Publications Director:** Susan White Sullivan
**Creative Art Director:** Gloria Bearden
**Photography Director:** Karen Hall
**Art Operations Director:** Jeff Curtis

PRODUCTION
**Managing Editor:** Mary Sullivan Hutcheson
**Production Editor:** Merrilee Gasaway
**Production Assistants:** Jo Ann Forrest and
  Janie Marie Wright

EDITORIAL
**Managing Editor:** Linda L. Trimble
**Senior Associate Editor:** Stacey Robertson Marshall
**Associate Editor:** Taryn L. Stewart

ART
**Senior Art Director:** Rhonda Shelby
**Senior Production Artist:** Lora Puls
**Production Artist:** Wendy Willets
**Color Technician:** Mark Hawkins
**Publishing Systems Administrator:** Becky Riddle
**Publishing Systems Assistants:** Myra S. Means and
  Chris Wertenberger

## BUSINESS STAFF

**Publisher:** Rick Barton
**Vice President, Finance:** Tom Siebenmorgen
**Vice President, Retail Marketing:** Bob Humphrey
**Director of Corporate Planning and Development:**
  Laticia Mull Cornett
**Vice President, National Accounts:** Pam Stebbins

**Retail Marketing Director:** Margaret Sweetin
**Vice President, Operations:** Jim Dittrich
**Comptroller for Operations:** Rob Thieme
**Retail Customer Service Manager:** Wanda Price
**Print Production Manager:** Fred F. Pruss

Softcover ISBN 1-57486-211-1

# TABLE OF CONTENTS

A TRIBUTE TO DICK MARTIN.................................................4

# A TRIBUTE TO DICK MARTIN

**W**ith his sparkling imagination and creative enthusiasm, Dick Martin amazed stitchers all over the world with his innovative plastic canvas designs. His passing earlier this year leaves his many fans to carry on the unique and beautiful designs that have, for many years, brought joy to crafters everywhere.

For over 25 years, the freelance artist designed a multitude of plastic canvas favorites for Leisure Arts. He earned his reputation as the "father" of three-dimensional plastic canvas while creating designs for almost 100 leaflets. He once said, "I think I have a touch of engineer in my blood, because I love to figure out how things go together."

Dick began his artistic career as a commercial artist illustrating and authoring children's educational books, games, and toys while working for several major publishing and advertising agencies. He later moved on to become a freelance designer for Avon Cosmetics, where he spent nearly 20 years designing children's jewelry and cosmetic products.

With all of that experience behind him, it was natural curiosity that first led Dick to design with plastic canvas. At the time (1968), many artists were experimenting with three-dimensional designs. "What magic it is when it works!" he once said. "Since plastic canvas holds such fascination for me, I have discovered many ways of using it which to this point have not been done."

Dick's creative designs caught the attention of Leisure Arts after he began attending meetings of the Embroiderers' Guild of America. He once laughingly remembered, "The first time I went to a meeting, there were 90 women and me. I was so scared, I had my wife take me! I think most of the women were

insulted, because they were accomplished cross stitchers and embroiderers, and no one was working with plastic canvas." He eventually started some of his fellow Guild members on plastic canvas projects. Soon after, he began designing projects for Leisure Arts.

Dick took much of his inspiration from nature, but he also enjoyed using images of toys and music boxes, along with Disney designs. Several trips to Disney World were great therapy for him. He once said,

"I come home filled with new ideas and feeling like a kid again."

Subject matter for full-time designers quickly becomes seasonal, according to Dick. And although he liked creating projects for all the holidays, he admitted that Christmas was his favorite. "The entire season is so full of symbolism. The possibilities are endless."

It was the pursuit of these "possibilities" that kept Dick designing, and he acknowledged that what he liked most about his work was the challenge. He wished for everyone who works with their hands the same joy and satisfaction that he felt during the creative process.

Looking back, Dick said he couldn't remember a time when he wasn't designing. He was once quoted as saying, "My first recollection [of designing] is coloring paper napkins and tablecloths in kindergarten. I was fortunate enough to have a teacher who encouraged my creativity."

Born February 19, 1931, in Hamburg, Iowa, a small town in the southwest corner of the state, Richard Allen Martin grew up surrounded by artistic influences. His mother and grandmother were both painters, and his brother won a scholarship to the American Academy of Art.

It was his love of design that led Dick to pursue an art degree from the University of Iowa, where his studies included silversmithing, fabric design, illustration, and layout. He said the four years of silversmithing offered a great experience in dimensional design. He explained, "It requires a great deal of patience, and so does needlepointing."

While in college, he met the woman who would become his wife of 48 years, Marjorie Kurtz, who was also an art major. "She's fabulous!" Dick once said enthusiastically. "She's my best critic and the reason I can do all I do. She makes it possible for me to concentrate my time on my creative work."

Dick resided in Tarrytown, New York, with Marjorie until his death on March 2, 2000. His three grown children carry on the tradition of creativity with various artistic interests, as does his wife, who continues to care for the extensive gardens that keep their yard colorful from early spring through late fall.

Dick Martin took on the design world with his creativity and zest for life, and he leaves behind a following that lovingly takes his imaginative designs into the new millennium.

Dick and his wife, Marjorie, are shown in 1990 relaxing in front of a playhouse they designed and built for their children.

# NATIVITY TRIPTYCH

*The whole family can share in the wonder of the Holy Birth with this simple Nativity triptych. With its three hinged panels illustrating that wondrous night, the scene will help show children the much-loved story of how the shepherds and Wise Men came to adore the Baby Jesus so many years ago. Family members can even take part by moving the freestanding sheep to kneel before the manger.*

Instructions on pages 34-36.

# SWEET KISSES

*Perfect as ornaments, wreath decorations, or gift embellishments, these cute characters are puckered up for sweet Christmas "kisses." Just pinch their cheeks for delicious chocolate surprises.*

Instructions on page 37.

# GINGERBOY BASKET

*With arms outstretched to carry lots of goodies, this whimsical gingerboy basket is a cute way to deliver a Yuletide surprise. The project is stitched on stiff canvas and is just the right size for an offering of yummy gingerbread cookies.*

Instructions on pages 38-41.

# TOUCH OF ELEGANCE

Gold beads and metallic thread make these miniature boxes exceptionally elegant. A dimensional tree on one box is easily created using two pieces of canvas, and a glittery bell ornament adds the final touch to the other.

Instructions on pages 42-43.

# BEAUTIFUL BOUTIQUES

*Sprinkle your home with holiday cheer —
decorate with these beautiful tissue box covers.
Embellished with metallic cord, beads, and
festive toppers, our Yuletide collection is sure
to add to the magic of Christmas.*

Instructions on pages 44-46.

# CHILDHOOD MEMORIES

This nostalgic magnet collection captures some of our favorite childhood memories of Christmas — ready-to-hug teddies, choo-choo trains, and jingling bells. What better way to bring the warmth of past holidays to every Yuletide celebration!

Mail Christmas Cards!

Instructions on page 47.

# JOLLY COUPLE

*Share the spirit of the season with these colorful projects featuring the jolly old elf himself — and Mrs. Claus, too! The delightful tree-trimmers will add a touch of merriment to your tree.*

Instructions on page 48.

13

# O HOLY NIGHT

*Fashioned in blue and white for a striking nighttime look, our elegant Nativity tissue box cover is studded with brilliant gold bead "stars." Metallic gold cord makes the Star of Bethlehem shine, and a musical button lets you celebrate the joy of the Savior's birth with a familiar carol.*

Instructions on pages 50-51.

# NORTH POLE FUN

*Adorning a festive boutique tissue box cover, our favorite Yuletide
visitor journeys through the snowy woods to deliver his holiday surprises.
The whimsical candy cane ornament also makes a novel bookmark.*

Instructions on pages 48-49.

# STUNNING POINSETTIA

*The legendary beauty of the poinsettia is elegantly captured on this lovely Christmas flowerpot cover. Embellished with golden highlights, the three-dimensional design is especially stunning when stitched against a snowy white background. Display a fresh poinsettia in this cheery holder to keep the festive spirit blooming all through the season.*

Instructions on page 55.

Instructions on pages 52-54.

# MAKE IT MERRY

*The merry motifs in this collection are sure to add sparkle to the
holidays. Stitched on 7 mesh canvas, the ten designs offer
bright ways to add Christmas cheer to a wreath.*

# DOOR DÉCOR SANTA

*You don't have to wait until Christmas Eve for a visit from the jolly old elf! Greet friends and family with our charming Santa door decoration that bears a merry holiday wish for all.*

Instructions on pages 56-60.

18

# GOODY BASKET BOUTIQUE

*This whimsical project for your Christmas kitchen stirs up a lot of holiday fun! A "basket" of tempting confections turns our boutique tissue box cover into a decoration (or gift!) that's sure to please. And it's wonderfully quick and easy to stitch.*

Instructions on page 61.

# GLORIOUS ANGEL

*Holding aloft a shining star, our charming angel topper makes a glorious finishing touch for the holiday tree. Lacy stitches and tiny pearl beads give the piece an airy, delicate appeal.*

Instructions on pages 62-65.

# ANGELIC MUSICIANS

*These precious angel ornaments create a symphony of beauty! Each seraph plays her own instrument, which is stitched in metallic braid. Shimmering beads add a heavenly sparkle to their robes and wings.*

Instructions on pages 66-68.

# DECK THE TREE

*Hang these colorful Christmas ornaments on your tree — or use them for package trims, wreath decorations, or even as merry magnets. They're so sweet (and simple to make!) that you'll easily come up with lots of fun holiday uses.*

Instructions on pages 72-73.

# SNOWY WOODLAND DÉCOR

*To bring a little of the outdoors into your home, try this festive woodland décor! Santa is joined by some of nature's cutest creatures to complete our three-dimensional scene, magnet set, and doorstop.*

Instructions on pages 74-80.

# MERRY SANTA

*Waving merrily from atop the tree, this cute fellow will add to the fun of the season. He's lightly stuffed, so he looks as "well-rounded" as the real Santa!*

Instructions on pages 82-83.

# SNOWMAN CARD HOLDER

*Let our chilly friend hold all your warm Christmas wishes! This striking accent is as decorative as it is useful — just fill his "pouch" with your special holiday greeting cards.*

Instructions on pages 84-87.

# HO-HO-HO TISSUE BOX

*With gifts gaily wrapped and under the tree, this pretty boutique tissue box cover is just right for someone who's "ho-ho-hoping" for something special from Santa. Topped with a chimney opening, the design features a snowy tree trimmed with French Knot ornaments.*

Instructions on page 81.

Instructions on pages 90-91

# TREETOP ANGEL BEAR

*You'll have a "beary" special Yuletide with this adorable angel bear atop your tree. With rosy heart cheeks and a dainty "lace" gown, our precious topper promises to add an angelic touch to your holiday decorating!*

# SNOWMAN CANISTER

*This frosty friend will bring lots of fun to your holiday table!
Dinner guests will love the cute standing snowman that bears
a surprise — his head lifts off so you can fill him with
candy or other treats for your friends to enjoy.*

Instructions on page 88-89.

# YULETIDE FAVORITES

*These Yuletide favorites embody the things we like best about Christmas.
The angel heralds the good news of Jesus' birth, the dove symbolizes
peace on earth, and Santa represents kindhearted generosity.*

Instructions on page 56.

# CANDY CANE SANTAS

*For charming kitchen décor, or for any spot that could use a touch of
Christmas spirit, these bright pieces capture the joy of the season!
The colorful door decoration, tissue box cover, and ornament
feature cute candy cane motifs and cheery smiles from
everyone's favorite gift-giver!*

Instructions on pages 69-71.

# NATIVITY TRIPTYCH

(Shown on pages 6-7.)
**Skill Level:** Intermediate
**Size:** 12½"w x 11¾"h
**Supplies:** Worsted weight yarn and Kreinik ⅛"w metallic gold ribbon (refer to color keys), three 10½" x 13½" sheets of clear 7 mesh plastic canvas, #16 tapestry needle, and posterboard.
**Stitches Used:** Backstitch, Cross Stitch, French Knot, Gobelin Stitch, Overcast Stitch, and Tent Stitch.

**Instructions:** Follow charts to cut and stitch Triptych pieces, working backstitches and French knots last. For supports, cut six pieces of posterboard slightly smaller than Center Back. Referring to photo, use tan overcast stitches to join Fronts along long edges. Using lt gold overcast stitches, join Backs along long edges. Join Fronts to Backs along top and side edges. Slide two posterboard supports into each point between Fronts and Backs. Join bottom edges of Fronts to Backs.

Referring to photo, glue Star to Center Front. Referring to photo, tack one Sheep Ear to each Sheep Side. With wrong sides together, match ▲'s and use matching color overcast stitches to join Sheep Side A to Sheep Side B. Referring to photo, tack Sheep to Sheep Base. Referring to photo, tack one Lamb Ear to each Lamb Side. With wrong sides together, match ♥'s and use matching color overcast stitches to join Lamb Side A to Lamb Side B. Referring to photo, tack Lamb to Lamb Base.

| COLOR | COLOR | COLOR |
|---|---|---|
| white | rust | black |
| lt gold | beige | metallic gold |
| peach | beige brown | *white |
| pink | dk beige brown | *orange |
| lt purple | lt tan | *white Fr. knot |
| purple | tan | *black Fr. knot |
| lt blue | brown | *Use 2 plies of yarn. |
| blue | dk brown | |

**Lamb Side A (10 x 13 threads)**

**Lamb Side B (13 x 10 threads)**

**Lamb Base (12 x 12 threads)**

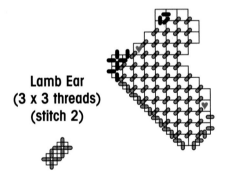

**Lamb Ear
(3 x 3 threads)
(stitch 2)**

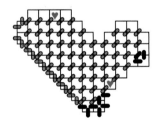

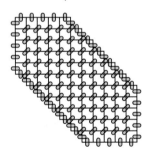

**Sheep Side A (13 x 16 threads)**

**Sheep Side B (16 x 13 threads)**

**Sheep Base (15 x 15 threads)**

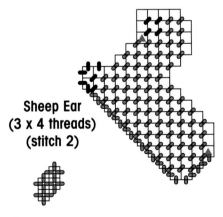

**Sheep Ear
(3 x 4 threads)
(stitch 2)**

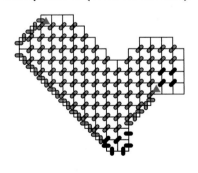

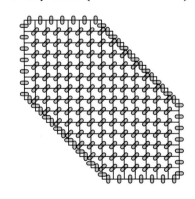

**Left Front/Back (28 x 65 threads) (cut 2) (stitch 1)**    **Center Front/Back (28 x 65 threads) (cut 2) (stitch 1)**

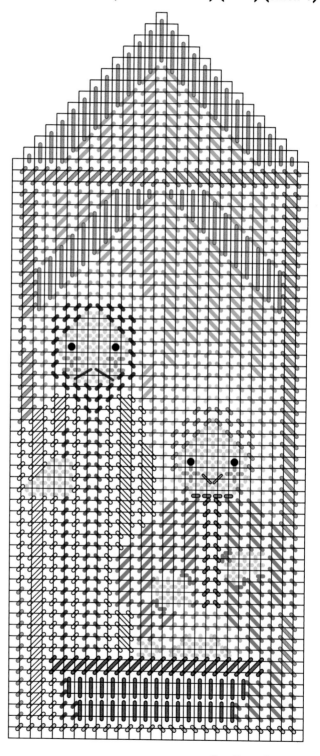

Continued on pg. 36.

| COLOR | COLOR |
|---|---|
| white | dk rust |
| lt gold | lt tan |
| gold | tan |
| peach | lt brown |
| pink | dk brown |
| orchid | black |
| vy lt purple | metallic gold |
| dk purple | *aqua Fr. knot |
| aqua | *black Fr. knot |
| lt green | *Use 2 plies of yarn. |
| green | |

**Right Front/Back (28 x 65 threads) (cut 2) (stitch 1)**

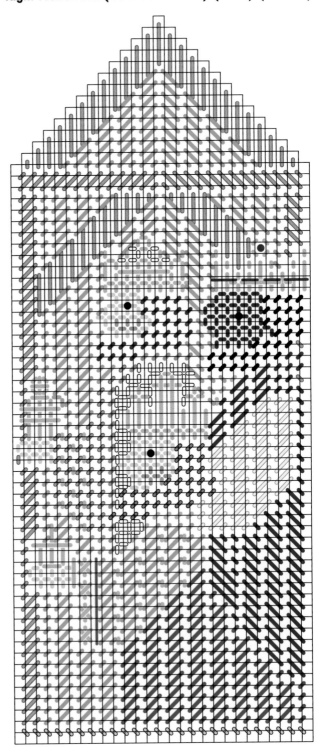

**Star (18 x 18 threads)**

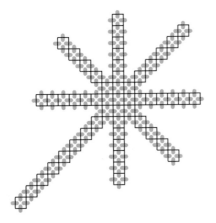

# SWEET KISSES

(Shown on page 8.)
**Skill Level:** Intermediate
**Size:** 3"w x 4"h each
**Supplies:** Worsted weight yarn (refer to color key), one 10½" x 13½" sheet of clear 7 mesh plastic canvas, and #16 tapestry needle.
**Stitches Used:** Backstitch, French Knot, Fringe Stitch, Gobelin Stitch, Overcast Stitch, and Tent Stitch.
**Instructions:** Follow charts to cut and stitch Reindeer or Santa pieces, working backstitches, French knots, and fringe stitches last. Referring to photo for yarn color, match ♥'s and use overcast stitches to join Top to Back along unworked threads. Matching ★'s, join Bottom to Back along unworked threads. For Santa, tack Holly to Santa Back.

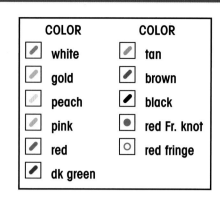

| COLOR | COLOR |
|---|---|
| white | tan |
| gold | brown |
| peach | black |
| pink | red Fr. knot |
| red | red fringe |
| dk green | |

**Reindeer Back (30 x 30 threads)**

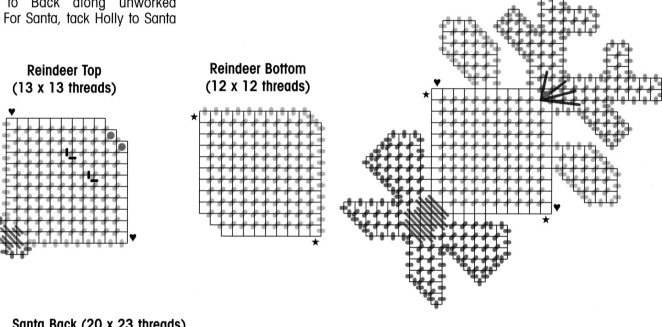

**Reindeer Top**
**(13 x 13 threads)**

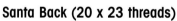

**Reindeer Bottom**
**(12 x 12 threads)**

**Santa Back (20 x 23 threads)**

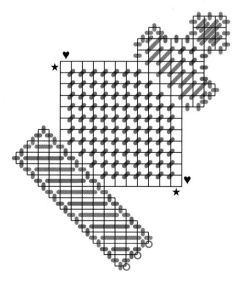

**Holly (8 x 8 threads)**

**Santa Top**
**(12 x 12 threads)**

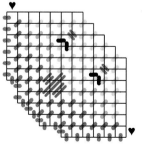

**Santa Bottom**
**(12 x 12 threads)**

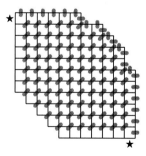

37

# GINGERBOY BASKET

(Shown on page 9.)

**Skill Level:** Intermediate

**Size:** 6"w x 9³/₄"h x 7¹/₂"d

**Supplies:** Worsted weight yarn or Needloft® Plastic Canvas Yarn (refer to color keys), five 10¹/₂" x 13¹/₂" sheets of clear 7 mesh stiff plastic canvas, #16 tapestry needle, and craft glue.

**Stitches Used:** Backstitch, Cross Stitch, French Knot, Gobelin Stitch, Overcast Stitch, and Tent Stitch.

**Instructions:** Follow charts to cut and stitch Basket pieces, working backstitches and French knots last. Using ecru overcast stitches, join Feet to Side A between ▲'s and ■'s through four thicknesses of canvas. Join Side B to Feet between ♦'s and ♣'s through four thicknesses of canvas. With wrong sides together, join Gingerbread Boy Front to Back between ★'s and ♥'s. Join remaining short edges of Side A and Side B to Gingerbread Boy Front and Back through four thicknesses of canvas. Using ecru overcast stitches, join Arm A to Side A between ▼'s through three thicknesses of canvas. Join Arm B to Side B between ♠'s through three thicknesses of canvas. Join Bottom to Gingerbread Boy Front and Back, Side A, Side B, and Feet through all thicknesses of plastic canvas. Cover remaining unworked edges of Basket. Using black overcast stitches, join Hat Front to Brim between ◗'s and ✖'s. Using ecru overcast stitches, cover bottom edge of Hat Back. Referring to photo for yarn color, join Hat Front to Back. Glue Hat to head. Tack Handle to Basket. Tack Arms to Handle.

**Hat Front/Back**
**(20 x 11 threads) (stitch 2)**

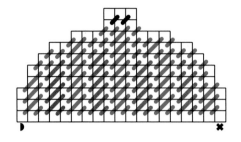

**Hat Brim**
**(20 x 6 threads)**

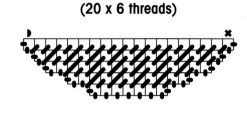

**Gingerbread Boy Front (38 x 56 threads)**

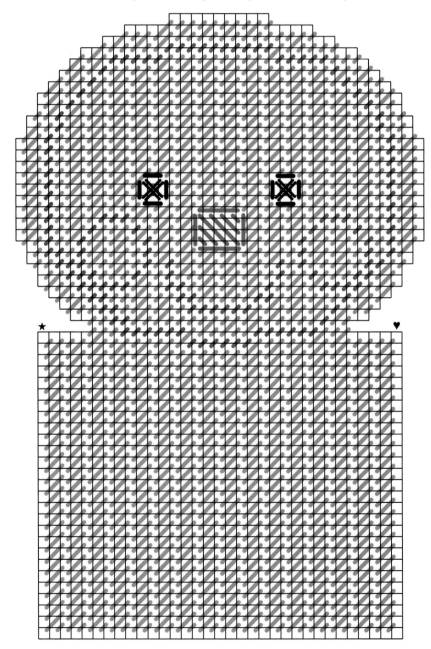

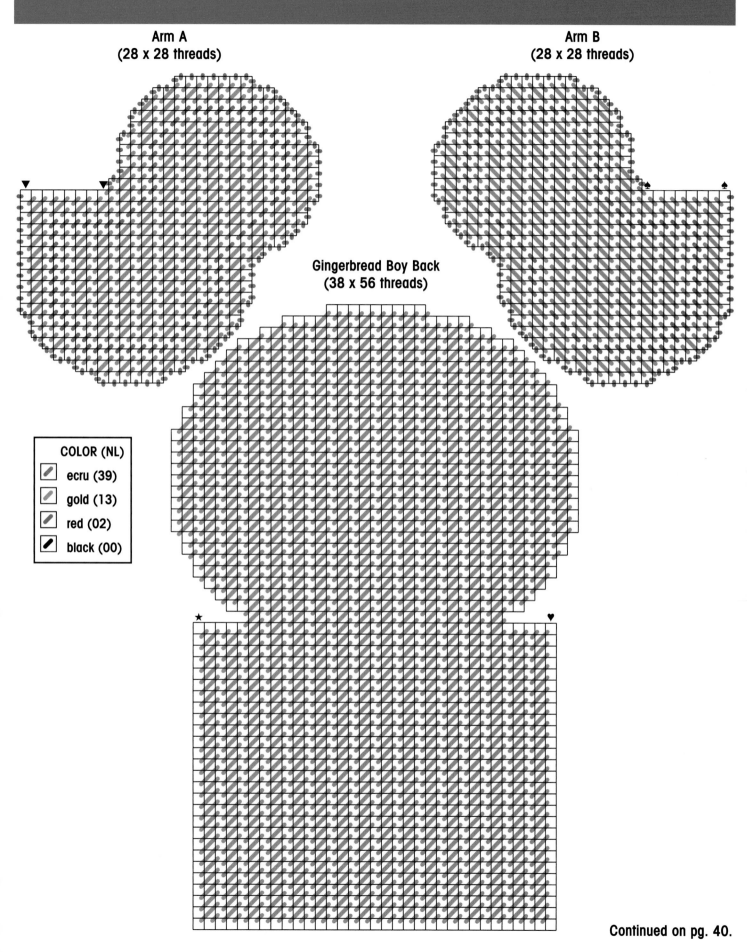

Arm A
(28 x 28 threads)

Arm B
(28 x 28 threads)

Gingerbread Boy Back
(38 x 56 threads)

COLOR (NL)
ecru (39)
gold (13)
red (02)
black (00)

Continued on pg. 40.

**COLOR (NL)**

- ✏ ecru (39)
- ✏ gold (13)
- ✏ red (02)
- ✏ black (00)
- ⬤ ecru (39) Fr. knot

**Side A (50 x 28 threads) (cut 2)**
Stack and stitch through two layers of canvas.

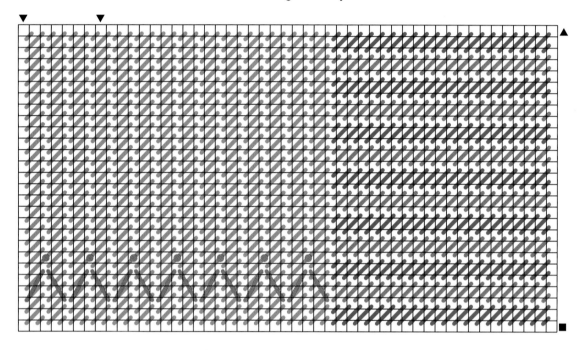

**Side B (50 x 28 threads) (cut 2)**
Stack and stitch through two layers of canvas.

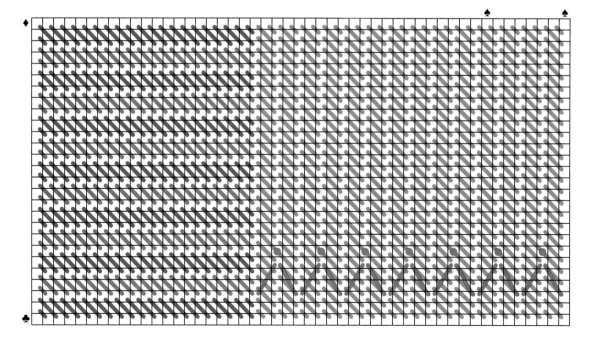

**Handle
(10 x 90 threads)**

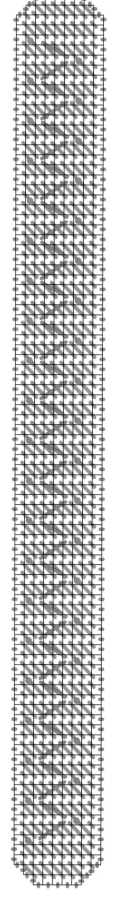

**Feet (34 x 32 threads) (cut 2)
Stack and stitch through two layers of canvas.**

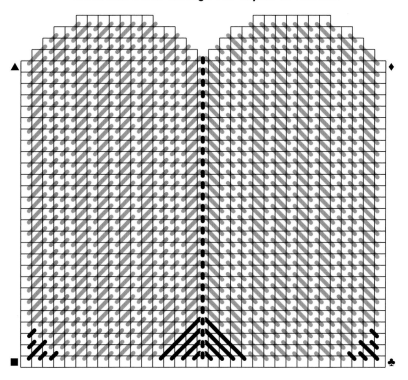

**Bottom (50 x 34 threads)**

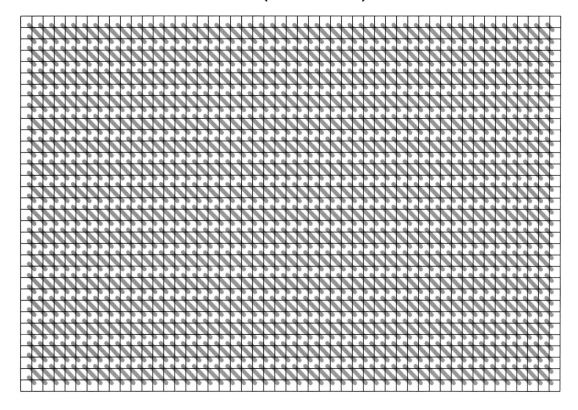

**TREE BOX**
(Shown on page 10.)
**Skill Level:** Intermediate
**Size:** 3¼"w x 4¼"h x 3¼"d
**Supplies:** Worsted weight yarn and metallic gold braid (refer to color key), one 10½" x 13½" sheet of clear 7 mesh plastic canvas, #16 tapestry needle, seventeen 4mm gold beads, and nylon thread and sewing needle.
**Stitches Used:** Cross Stitch, Gobelin Stitch, Overcast Stitch, Scotch Stitch, and Tent Stitch.

**Instructions:** Follow charts to cut and stitch Box pieces, leaving stitches in shaded areas unworked. Using matching color overcast stitches, join Box Sides along short edges. Work stitches in pink shaded area to join Box Sides to Bottom. Using ecru overcast stitches, join Box Top Sides along short edges. Work stitches in blue shaded area to join Box Top Sides to Top. Referring to photo, slide Tree Sides together and tack in place. Tack Tree to Box Top.

| COLOR | |
|---|---|
| ✏ | ecru |
| ✏ | green |
| ✏ | brown |
| ✏ | metallic gold |
| ⬤ | bead placement |

**Tree Side #1**
**(15 x 15 threads)**

**Tree Box Top Side**
**(18 x 4 threads) (stitch 4)**

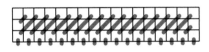

**Tree Box Side**
**(20 x 12 threads) (stitch 4)**

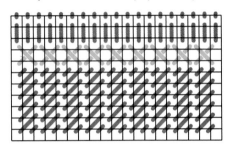

**Tree Side #2**
**(15 x 15 threads)**

**Tree Box Top**
**(22 x 22 threads)**

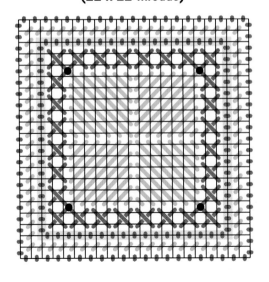

**Tree Box Bottom**
**(22 x 22 threads)**

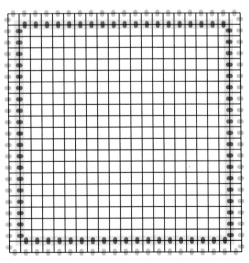

## BELL BOX

(Shown on page 10.)
**Skill Level:** Intermediate
**Size:** 3¼"w x 2"h x 3¼"d
**Supplies:** Worsted weight yarn and metallic gold braid (refer to color key), one 10½" x 13½" sheet of clear 7 mesh plastic canvas, #16 tapestry needle, 12" length of ⅜"w red ribbon, six 4mm gold beads, nylon thread and sewing needle, and craft glue.
**Stitches Used:** Backstitch, Cross Stitch, French Knot, Gobelin Stitch, Overcast Stitch, Scotch Stitch, and Tent Stitch.

**Instructions:** Follow charts to cut and stitch Box pieces, working backstitches and French knots last and leaving stitches in shaded areas unworked. Using matching color overcast stitches, join Box Sides along short edges. Work stitches in yellow shaded area to join Box Sides to Bottom. Using green overcast stitches, join Box Top Sides along short edges. Work stitches in pink shaded area to join Box Top Sides to Top. Tie ribbon into bow and trim ends. Glue bow to Box Top. Glue Bell to Box Top.

| COLOR | |
|---|---|
| ✏ | ecru |
| ✏ | red |
| ✏ | green |
| ✏ | metallic gold |
| ✏ | *green |
| ● | red Fr. knot |
| ⬤ | bead placement |
| *Use 2 plies of yarn. | |

**Bell**
**(8 x 8 threads)**

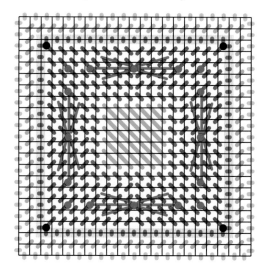

**Bell Box Top Side**
**(18 x 4 threads) (stitch 4)**

**Bell Box Side**
**(20 x 12 threads) (stitch 4)**

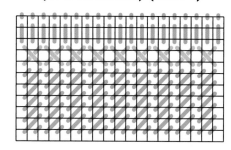

**Bell Box Top**
**(22 x 22 threads)**

**Bell Box Bottom**
**(22 x 22 threads)**

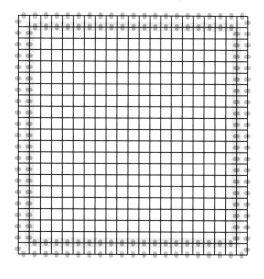

## HOLLY TISSUE BOX COVER

(Shown on page 11.)
**Skill Level:** Beginner
**Size:** 4³/₄"w x 5³/₄"h x 4³/₄"d
*(Fits a 4¹/₄"w x 5¹/₄"h x 4¹/₄"d boutique tissue box.)*
**Supplies:** Worsted weight yarn or Needloft® Plastic Canvas Yarn and 5mm metallic gold cord (refer to color key), two 10¹/₂" x 13¹/₂" sheets of white 7 mesh plastic canvas, and #16 tapestry needle.
**Stitches Used:** Backstitch, Cross Stitch, Gobelin Stitch, Overcast Stitch, and Tent Stitch.
**Instructions:** Follow charts to cut and stitch Tissue Box Cover pieces, working backstitches last. Using white overcast stitches, join Sides along long edges. Join Top to Sides.

| COLOR (NL) | |
|---|---|
| ⬜ | white (41) |
| ✏ | red (02) |
| ✏ | green (53) |
| ⬜ | metallic gold |

**Side (32 x 38 threads) (stitch 4)**

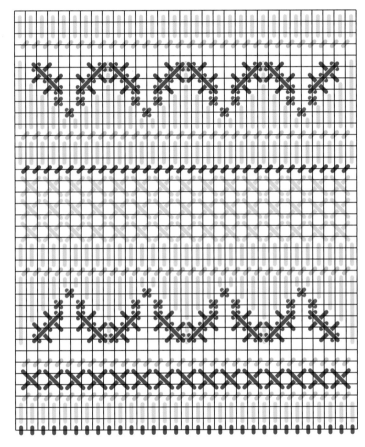

**Top (32 x 32 threads)**

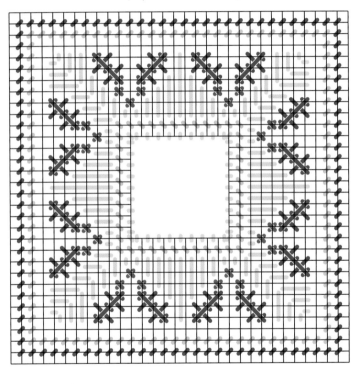

## SILVER BELL TISSUE BOX COVER

(Shown on page 11.)
**Skill Level:** Intermediate
**Size:** 5¹/₂"w x 7³/₄"h x 5¹/₂"d
*(Fits a 4¹/₄"w x 5¹/₄"h x 4¹/₄"d boutique tissue box.)*
**Supplies:** Worsted weight yarn or Needloft® Plastic Canvas Yarn and 5mm metallic silver cord, (refer to color key), two 10¹/₂" x 13¹/₂" sheets of white 7 mesh plastic canvas, #16 tapestry needle, 60" of ³/₈"w red satin ribbon, white tissue paper, 1¹/₂" dia. music button (ours plays "Silver Bells"), 108 –

5mm silver beads, nylon thread and sewing needle, and craft glue.
**Stitches Used:** Backstitch, Cross Stitch, French Knot, Gobelin Stitch, Overcast Stitch, and Tent Stitch.
**Instructions:** Follow charts to cut and stitch Tissue Box Cover pieces, working backstitches and French knots last. Use nylon thread and sewing needle to attach one bead at each ▲ on Top and Bells. With right sides together, match ■'s and use white overcast stitches to join Foliage pieces to Top. Tack corners of Foliage together. Using white overcast

stitches, join Sides along long edges. Join Top to Sides. Matching ★'s, tack one Bell to one Side at ★'s. Glue music button between Bell and Side. Matching ★'s, tack remaining Bells to Sides. Place tissue paper between Bells and Sides. Cut four 4" lengths of ribbon. Referring to photo, thread one length of ribbon through top of each bell. Glue ribbon ends together at bottom of Foliage. Cut four 11" lengths of ribbon. Tie each length of ribbon in a bow and trim ends. Referring to photo, glue bows to Foliage.

## COLOR (NL)

- white (41)
- green (53)
- metallic silver
- ● red (02) Fr. knot
- ▲ silver bead placement

### Foliage
### (14 x 14 threads)
### (stitch 4)

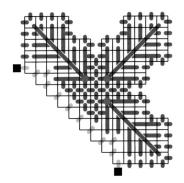

### Bell (28 x 28 threads)
### (stitch 4)

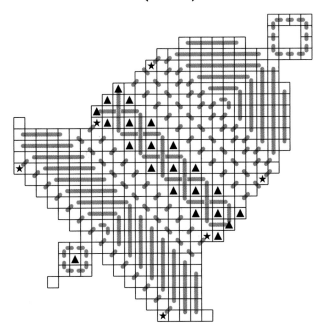

## Top (32 x 32 threads)

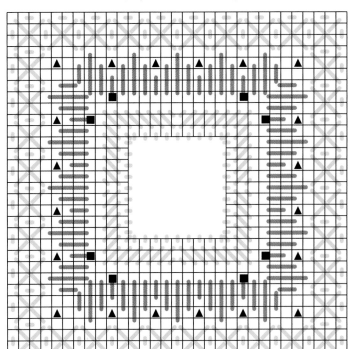

## Side (32 x 38 threads) (stitch 4)

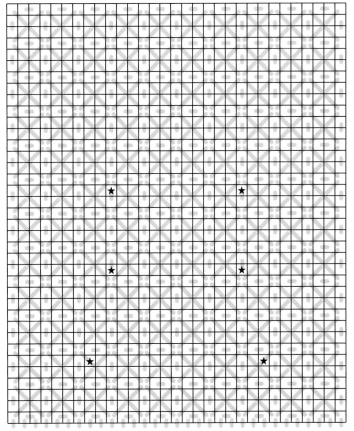

Continued on pg. 46.

## CANDY CANE TISSUE BOX COVER

(Shown on page 11.)

**Skill Level:** Beginner

**Size:** 4³/₄"w x 5¹/₂"h x 4³/₄"d

*(Fits a 4¹/₄"w x 5¹/₄"h x 4¹/₄"d boutique tissue box.)*

**Supplies:** Worsted weight yarn or Needloft® Plastic Canvas Yarn (refer to color key), two 10¹/₂" x 13¹/₂" sheets of white 7 mesh plastic canvas, #16 tapestry needle, and craft glue.

**Stitches Used:** Backstitch, Gobelin Stitch, Overcast Stitch, and Tent Stitch.

**Instructions:** Follow charts to cut and stitch Tissue Box Cover pieces, working backstitches last. Using green overcast stitches, join Sides along long edges. Using white overcast stitches, join Top to Sides. Matching ★'s, glue Leaves to Top. Matching ■'s, glue Peppermints to Top and Sides.

| COLOR (NL) | |
|---|---|
| | white (41) |
| ✎ | red (02) |
| ✎ | green (53) |

**Leaves (12 x 9 threads) (stitch 4)**

**Peppermint (8 x 8 threads) (stitch 12)**

**Side (32 x 38 threads) (stitch 4)**

**Top (32 x 32 threads)**

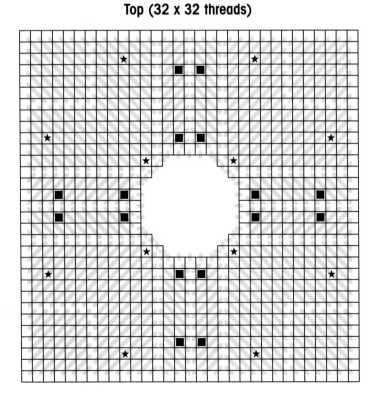

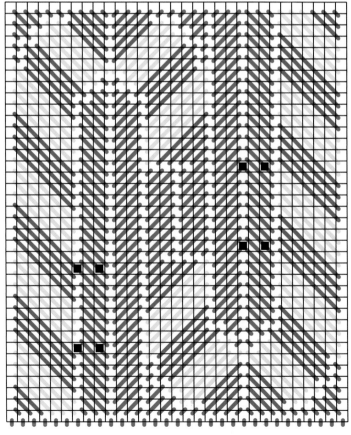

# CHILDHOOD MEMORIES

(Shown on page 12.)

**Skill Level:** Beginner

**Approx. Size:** 2³/₄"w x 3"h each

**Supplies:** Worsted weight yarn and Kreinik heavy #32 metallic gold braid (refer to color key), one 10¹/₂" x 13¹/₂" sheet of clear 7 mesh plastic canvas, #16 tapestry needle, magnetic strip, and craft glue.

**Stitches Used:** Backstitch, Cross Stitch, French Knot, Overcast Stitch, Reversed Tent Stitch, and Tent Stitch.

**Instructions:** Follow chart to cut and stitch desired Magnet, working backstitches and French knots last. Glue magnetic strip to wrong side of Magnet.

| COLOR | COLOR | COLOR |
|---|---|---|
| white | green | †pink Fr. knot |
| yellow | beige | red Fr. knot |
| gold | tan | green Fr. knot |
| pink | brown | black Fr. knot |
| red | black | metallic gold Fr. knot |
| purple | metallic gold | *Use 2 strands of braid. |
| blue | *metallic gold | †Use 2 plies of yarn. |
| lt green | †green | |

**Dog (21 x 21 threads)**

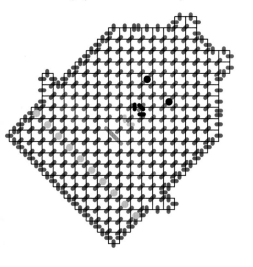

**Candle (17 x 16 threads)**

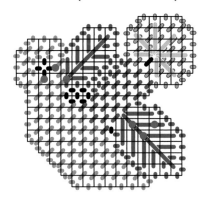

**Cat (19 x 21 threads)**

**Train (24 x 21 threads)**

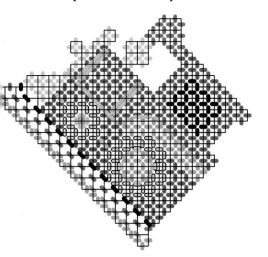

**Bell (16 x 16 threads)**

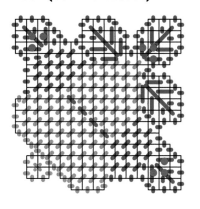

**Bear (21 x 21 threads)**

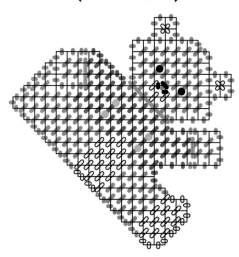

# JOLLY COUPLE

(Shown on page 13.)
**Skill Level:** Beginner
**Approx. Size:** 4¹/₂"w x 4¹/₂"h each
**Supplies:** Worsted weight yarn and Rainbow Gallery metallic gold yarn (refer to color key), one 10¹/₂" x 13¹/₂" sheet of clear 7 mesh plastic canvas, #16 tapestry needle, and nylon thread.
**Stitches Used:** Backstitch, Cross Stitch, French Knot, Gobelin Stitch, Overcast Stitch, Smyrna Cross Stitch, and Tent Stitch.
**Instructions:** Follow charts to cut and stitch Ornaments, working backstitches and French knots last. For hanger, thread 8" length of nylon thread through top of each Ornament. Knot ends of nylon thread 3″ above Ornaments; trim ends.

| COLOR | | COLOR | |
|---|---|---|---|
| ⟋ | white | ⟋ | metallic gold |
| ⟋ | flesh | ⟋ | *red |
| ⟋ | pink | ☐ | red Fr. knot |
| ⟋ | red | ● | *red Fr. knot |
| ⟋ | purple | ● | *green Fr. knot |
| ⟋ | green | ● | *black Fr. knot |
| ⟋ | tan | ● | metallic gold Fr. knot |
| ⟋ | black | | *Use 2 plies of yarn. |

**Mrs. Claus Ornament (28 x 30 threads)**

**Santa Ornament (30 x 31 threads)**

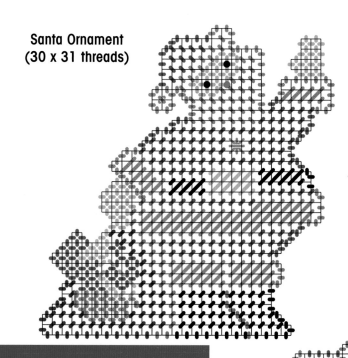

# NORTH POLE FUN

**CANDY CANE ORNAMENT & TISSUE BOX COVER**
(Shown on page 15.)
**Skill Level:** Beginner
**Ornament Size:** 4¹/₂"w x 4¹/₂"h
**Tissue Box Cover Size:** 4³/₄"w x 6³/₄"h x 4³/₄"d
(Cover fits a 4¹/₄"w x 5¹/₄"h x 4¹/₄"d boutique tissue box.)
**Supplies:** Worsted weight yarn (refer to color key), two 10¹/₂" x 13¹/₂" sheets of clear 7 mesh plastic canvas, #16 tapestry needle, and nylon thread.
**Stitches Used:** Backstitch, Cross Stitch, French Knot, Gobelin Stitch, Overcast Stitch, and Tent Stitch.
**Instructions:** Follow charts to cut and stitch Ornament and Tissue Box Cover pieces, working backstitches and French knots last. Use matching color overcast stitches for all joining. With right sides together, match ■'s to join Hat Back to Top. Join Sides and Front along long edges. Join Top and Hat Back to Sides and Front. For Ornament hanger, thread 8" length of nylon thread through top of Ornament. Knot ends of nylon thread 3″ above Ornament; trim ends.

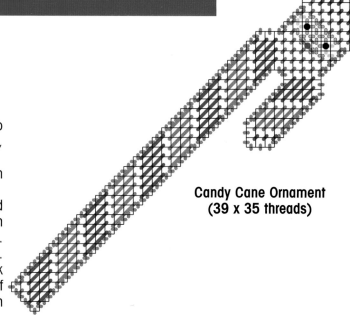

**Candy Cane Ornament (39 x 35 threads)**

## COLOR

| | | | | | | |
|---|---|---|---|---|---|---|
| ▨ | white | ▨ | purple | ▨ | *red | |
| ▨ | yellow | ▨ | lt blue | ⊙ | white Fr. knot | |
| ▨ | orange | ▨ | blue | ⊙ | dk pink Fr. knot | |
| ▨ | flesh | ▨ | lt green | ● | *red Fr. knot | |
| ▨ | pink | ▨ | green | ⬤ | *black Fr. knot | |
| ▨ | dk pink | ▨ | tan | *Use 2 plies of yarn. | | |
| ▨ | red | ▨ | black | | | |

## Top (32 x 32 threads)

### Hat Back (19 x 8 threads)

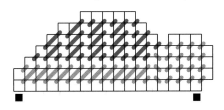

### Front (32 x 45 threads)

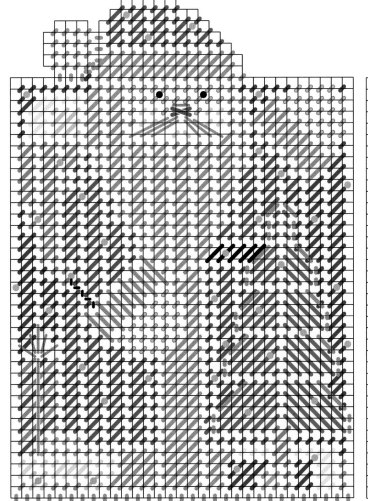

## Side (32 x 38 threads) (stitch 3)
### Complete background with blue
### Gobelin stitches as indicated on chart.

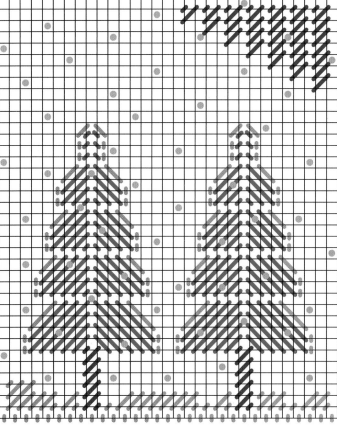

# O HOLY NIGHT

(Shown on page 14.)
**Skill Level:** Intermediate
**Size:** 4³/₄"w x 7"h x 4³/₄"d
*(Fits a 4¹/₄"w x 5¹/₄"h x 4¹/₄"d boutique tissue box.)*
**Supplies:** Worsted weight yarn or Needloft® Plastic Canvas Yarn and metallic gold cord (refer to color key), two 10¹/₂" x 13¹/₂" sheets of clear 7 mesh plastic canvas, two 10¹/₂" x 13¹/₂" sheets of white 7 mesh plastic canvas, #16 tapestry needle, 143 – 3mm round gold beads, two 12mm gold sequins, one 8mm gold sequin, nylon thread and sewing needle, music button, and craft glue.
**Stitches Used:** Backstitch, Gobelin Stitch, Overcast Stitch, and Tent Stitch.
**Instructions:** Cut Nativity, Trees, and Staff from white plastic canvas. Cut remaining pieces from clear plastic canvas. Follow charts to stitch Tissue Box Cover pieces. Use nylon thread to sew beads to pieces. Referring to photo, glue sequins to wrong side of Nativity. Referring to photo, use nylon thread to tack Trees, Staff, and Nativity to Sides. Use blue overcast stitches for all joining. With right sides together, match ■'s to join Backs to Base. With right sides facing inward, join Inner Sides along short edges. Matching ▲'s, join Inner Sides to wrong side of Top. With right sides facing outward, join Outer Sides along short edges. Matching ♦'s, join Outer Sides to Base. Glue music button to Base at ♥. Placing music button under gold star on Top, join Top to Outer Sides. Join Inner Sides to Base. Join Sides to Base and Backs. Join Sides along unworked edges.

| COLOR (NL) | |
|---|---|
| ✎ | white (41) |
| ✎ | blue (32) |
| ✎ | metallic gold |
| ● | bead placement |

**Inner Side (10 x 4 threads) (stitch 4)**

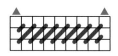

**Outer Side (26 x 4 threads) (stitch 4)**

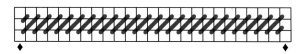

**Side (32 x 47 threads) (stitch 4)**

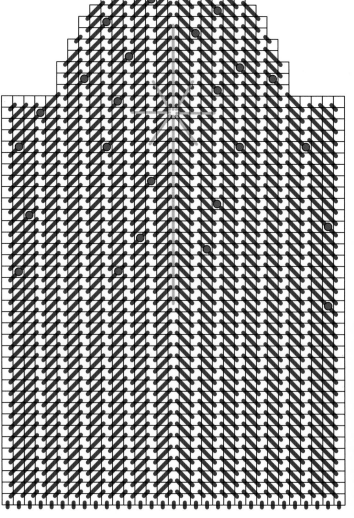

**Base (32 x 32 threads)**

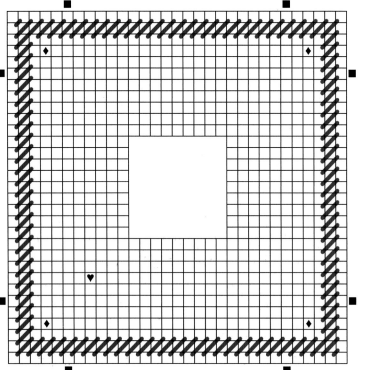

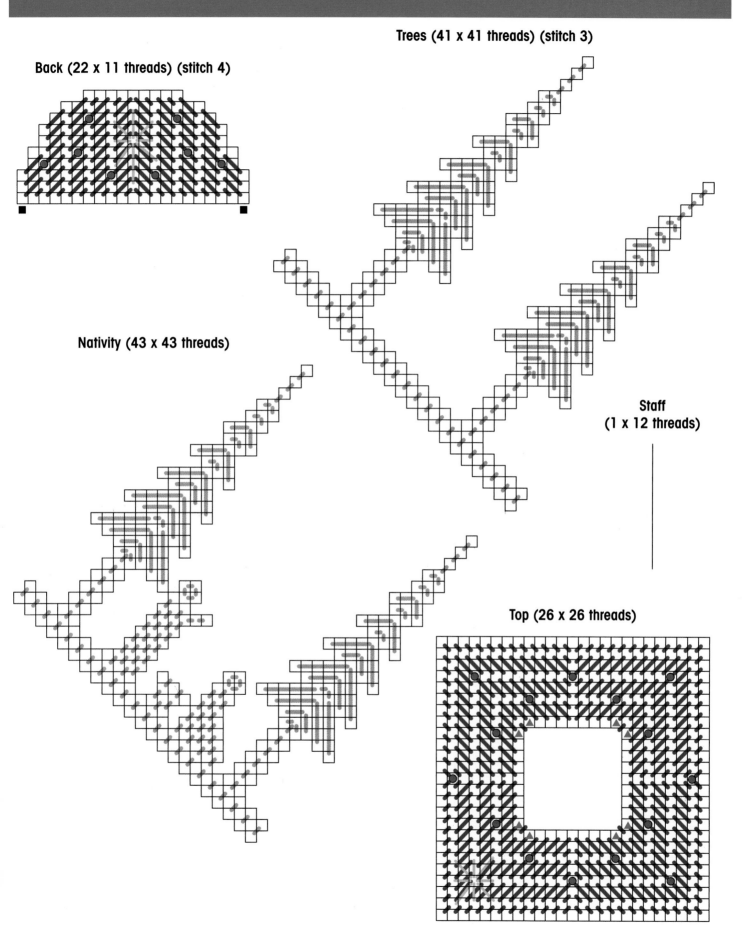

**Trees (41 x 41 threads) (stitch 3)**

**Back (22 x 11 threads) (stitch 4)**

**Nativity (43 x 43 threads)**

**Staff
(1 x 12 threads)**

**Top (26 x 26 threads)**

(Shown on page 17.)
**Skill Level:** Beginner
**Approx. Size:** 4³/₄"w x 4¹/₄"h each
**Supplies:** Worsted weight yarn and Kreinik medium #16 metallic gold braid (refer to color keys), one 10¹/₂" x 13¹/₂" sheet of clear 7 mesh plastic, #16 tapestry needle, nylon thread and sewing needle, and craft glue.
*For Gingerbread House only:* 8" length of ¹/₁₆"w red satin ribbon.
**Stitches Used:** Backstitch, Cross Stitch, French Knot, Gobelin Stitch, Mosaic Stitch, Overcast Stitch, Scotch Stitch, and Tent Stitch.

**Instructions:** Follow chart(s) to cut and stitch desired Ornament, working backstitches and French knots last. (Note: Use two strands of metallic braid for good coverage.) For hanger, thread 8" length of nylon thread through top of Ornament. Knot ends of nylon thread 3" above Ornament; trim ends.
*For Angel only:* Cut a 2" length of metallic gold braid and fold in half. Referring to photo, glue folded end of braid to wrong side of Angel and loose ends to wrong side of Heart.
*For Bell only:* Referring to photo, glue Large Leaves to Bell.

*For Candy Cane only:* Referring to photo, thread an 8" length of green yarn through stitched piece. Tie yarn in a bow and trim ends.
*For Gingerbread House only:* Tie ribbon in a bow and trim ends. Glue bow to Wreath. Referring to photo, glue Wreath to Gingerbread House.
*For Star only:* Referring to photo, tack Leaves to Star.
*For Santa only:* Referring to photo, glue Small Leaves to Santa.

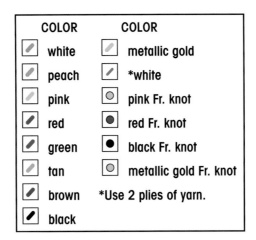

| COLOR | COLOR |
|---|---|
| white | metallic gold |
| peach | *white |
| pink | pink Fr. knot |
| red | red Fr. knot |
| green | black Fr. knot |
| tan | metallic gold Fr. knot |
| brown | *Use 2 plies of yarn. |
| black | |

**Train (32 x 25 threads)**

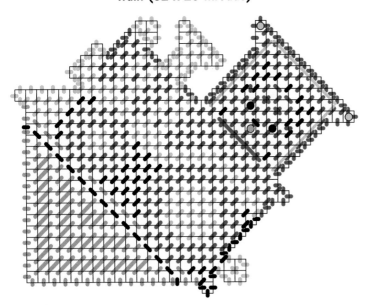

**Tree (25 x 25 threads)**

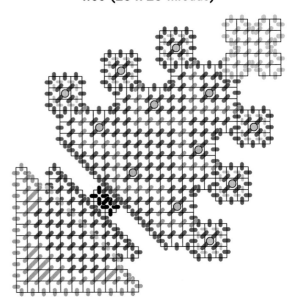

### Heart (5 x 5 threads)

### Small Leaves (8 x 5 threads)

### Angel (25 x 25 threads)

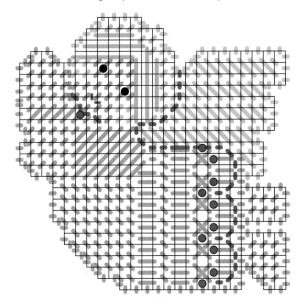

### Santa (28 x 25 threads)

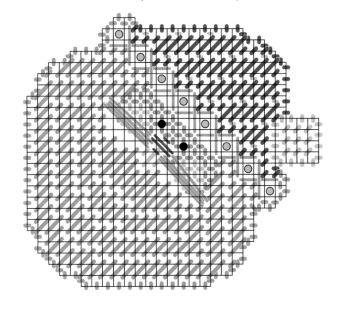

### Wreath (5 x 5 threads)

### Leaf (6 x 6 threads) (stitch 4)

### Gingerbread House (28 x 28 threads)

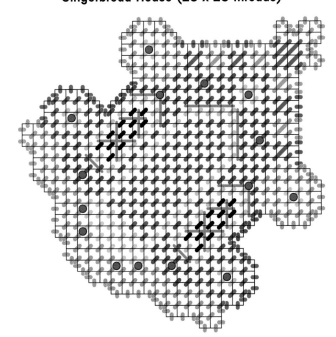

### Star (27 x 27 threads)

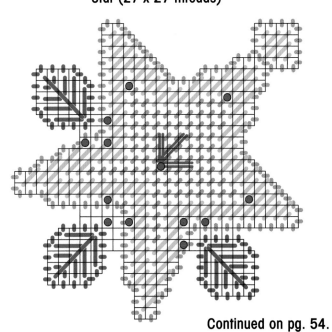

**Continued on pg. 54.**

| COLOR | COLOR |
|---|---|
| white | black |
| pink | metallic gold |
| red | red Fr. knot |
| green | green Fr. knot |
| tan | black Fr. knot |
| brown | metallic gold Fr. knot |

**Large Leaves (10 x 8 threads) (stitch 2)**

**Candy Cane (25 x 27 threads)**

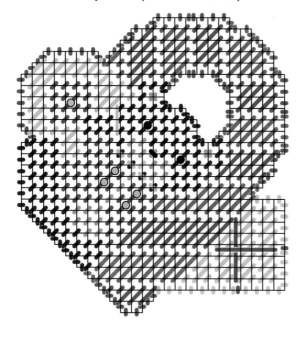

**Bell (25 x 25 threads)**

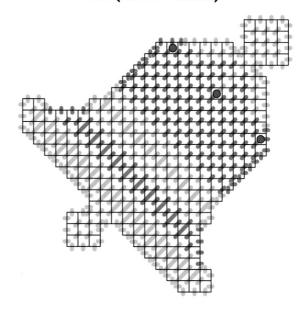

**Horse (28 x 29 threads)**

**Candle (26 x 26 threads)**

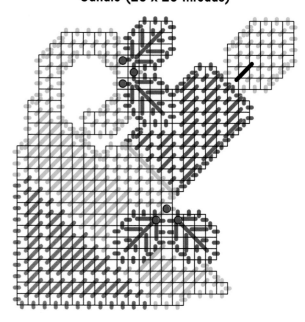

# STUNNING POINSETTIA

(Shown on page 16.)
**Skill Level:** Intermediate
**Size:** 5³/₈"h x 6¹/₂" dia
**Supplies:** Worsted weight yarn and Rainbow Gallery metallic gold yarn (refer to color key), one 13¹/₂" x 22¹/₂" sheet of clear 7 mesh plastic canvas, #16 tapestry needle, and a 5¹/₄"h x 6" dia. white planter.
**Stitches Used:** Backstitch, French Knot, Gobelin Stitch, Overcast Stitch, and Tent Stitch.
**Instructions:** For Side, cut a piece of canvas 137 x 36 threads. Follow Side chart to center and stitch poinsettia design on Side. Follow charts to work Poinsettia Center and remainder of Side, working backstitches and French knots last and leaving stitches in pink shaded areas unworked. Matching ★'s, work stitches in pink shaded areas to join ends of Side, forming a cylinder. Use white overcast stitches to cover unworked edges. Matching ♦'s, tack Poinsettia Center to Side.

| COLOR | |
|---|---|
| 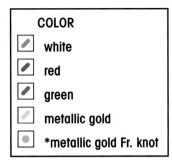 | white |
| | red |
| | green |
| | metallic gold |
| | *metallic gold Fr. knot |

**Poinsettia Center (16 x 16 threads)**

**Side (137 x 36 threads)**

Repeat          Repeat

# YULETIDE FAVORITES

(Shown on page 31.)
**Skill Level:** Beginner
**Approx. Size:** 2³/₄"w x 3"h each
**Supplies:** Worsted weight yarn or Needloft® Plastic Canvas Yarn, embroidery floss, and metallic gold braid (refer to color key); one 10¹/₂" x 13¹/₂" sheet of clear 7 mesh plastic canvas; #16 tapestry needle; magnetic strip; and craft glue.
**Stitches Used:** Backstitch, Cross Stitch, French Knot, Gobelin Stitch, Overcast Stitch, and Tent Stitch.
**Instructions:** Follow chart to cut and stitch desired magnet, working backstitches and French knots last. Glue magnetic strip to wrong side of magnet.

| COLOR (NL) | | COLOR (NL) | |
|---|---|---|---|
| ⬭ | white (41) | ⬭ | *metallic gold |
| ⬭ | flesh (56) | ⬭ | †orange |
| ⬭ | pink (08) | ● | red (02) Fr. knot |
| ⬭ | red (02) | ● | †black Fr. knot |
| ⬭ | green (27) | ◉ | metallic gold Fr. knot |
| ⬭ | rust (10) | *Use 2 strands of braid. | |
| ⬭ | metallic gold | †Use 6 strands of floss. | |

**Dove (18 x 18 threads)**

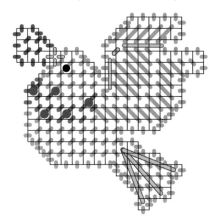

**Angel (17 x 17 threads)**

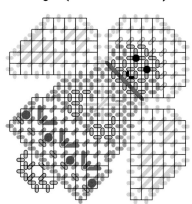

**Santa (17 x 18 threads)**

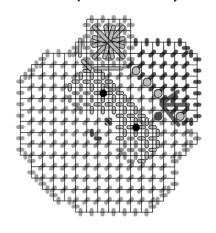

# DOOR DÉCOR SANTA

(Shown on page 18.)
**Skill Level:** Intermediate
**Size:** 18¹/₂"w x 32"h
**Supplies:** Worsted weight yarn and Kreinik ¹/₈"w gold metallic ribbon (refer to color keys), five 10¹/₂" x 13¹/₂" sheets of clear 7 mesh plastic canvas, #16 tapestry needle, sewing needle and thread, sawtooth hanger, and craft glue.
**Stitches Used:** Backstitch, Cross Stitch, French Knot, Gobelin Stitch, Overcast Stitch, and Tent Stitch.
**Instructions:** Follow charts to cut and stitch Door Decoration pieces, working backstitches and French knots last and leaving shaded areas unworked. Stitches with dots extending from them should be worked as one long stitch across pieces of canvas. Matching ♥'s, work stitches in shaded area through two thicknesses of canvas to join Pom-pom to Section A. Referring to photo, glue Holly Leaves to Section A. Referring to photo, glue Button to Section B. Matching ★'s, place Section A on top of Section B. Matching ▲'s, place Sections A and B on top of Section D. Work stitches in shaded areas through all thicknesses to join Sections A, B, and D. Matching ♣'s, place Section B on top of Section C. Matching ♦'s, place Sections B and C on top of Section E. Work stitches in shaded areas through all thicknesses to join Sections B, C, and E. For hanger, sew sawtooth hanger to back of stitched piece.

**Diagram**

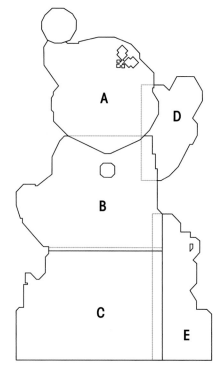

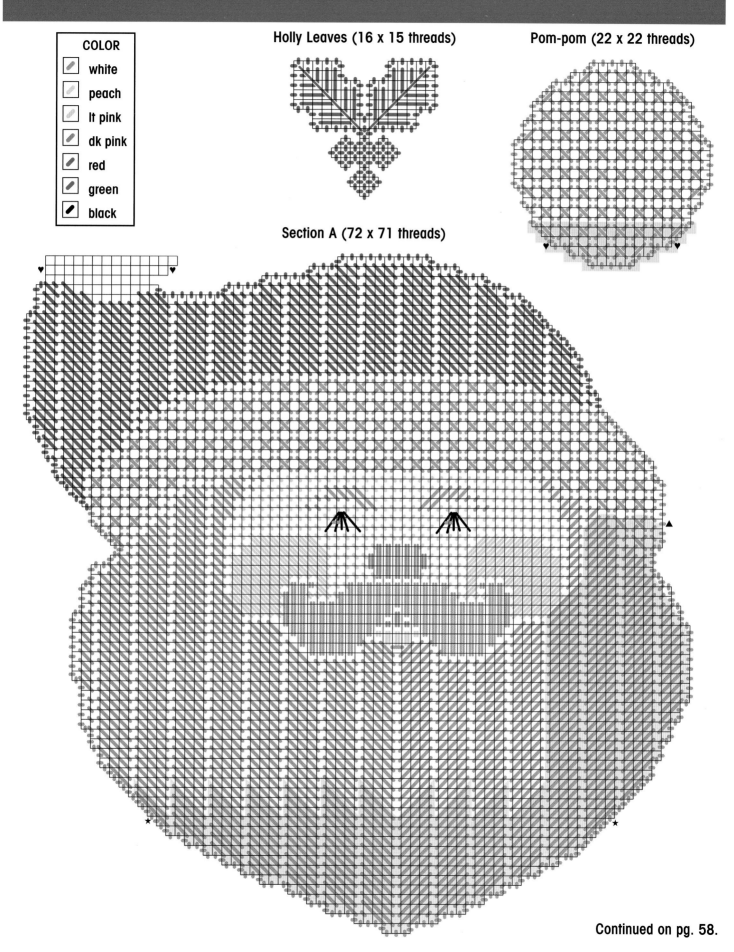

COLOR

- white
- peach
- lt pink
- dk pink
- red
- green
- black

Holly Leaves (16 x 15 threads)

Pom-pom (22 x 22 threads)

Section A (72 x 71 threads)

Continued on pg. 58.

**Section B (91 x 71 threads)**

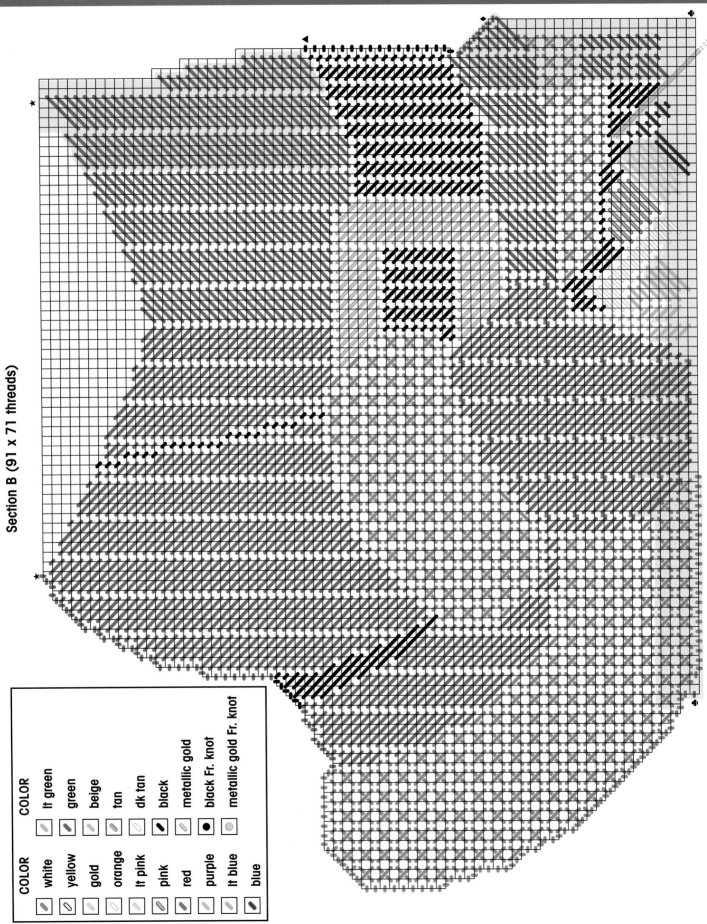

| COLOR | | COLOR | |
|---|---|---|---|
| white | | lt green | |
| yellow | | green | |
| gold | | beige | |
| orange | | tan | |
| lt pink | | dk tan | |
| pink | | black | |
| red | | metallic gold | |
| purple | | black Fr. knot | |
| lt blue | | metallic gold Fr. knot | |
| blue | | | |

Section C (91 x 71 threads)

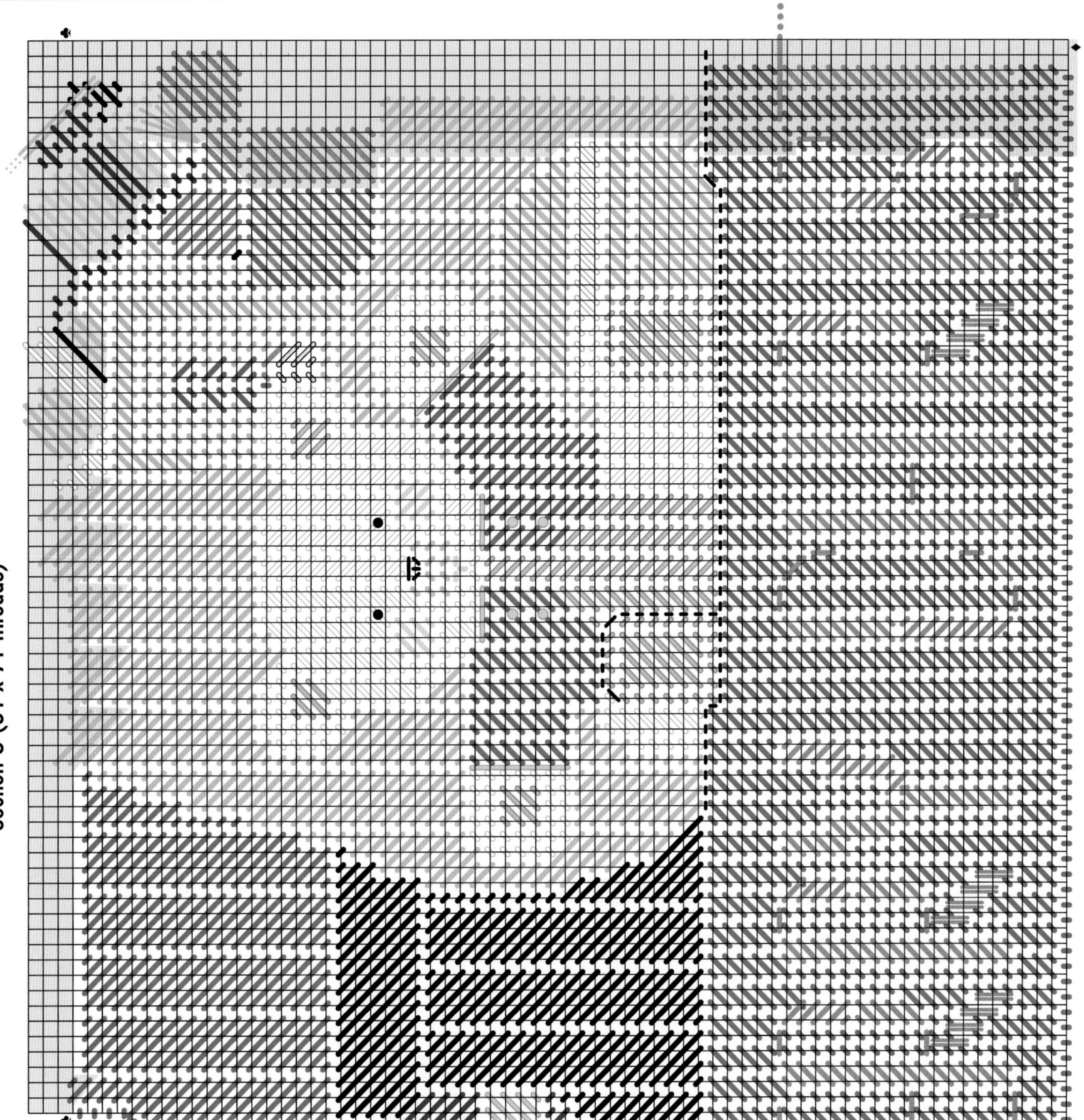

Button (10 x 10 threads)

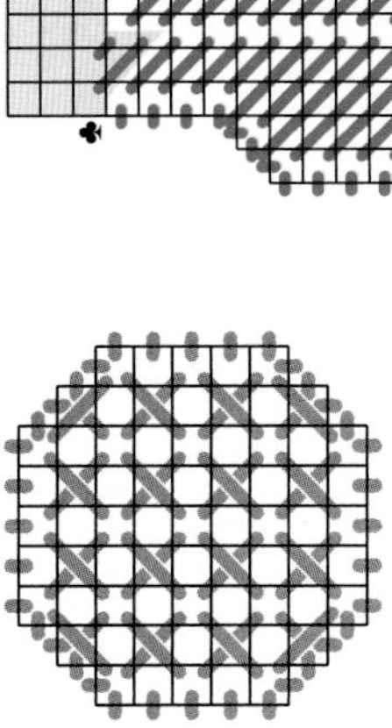

Continued on pg. 60.

**Section E (38 x 90 threads)**

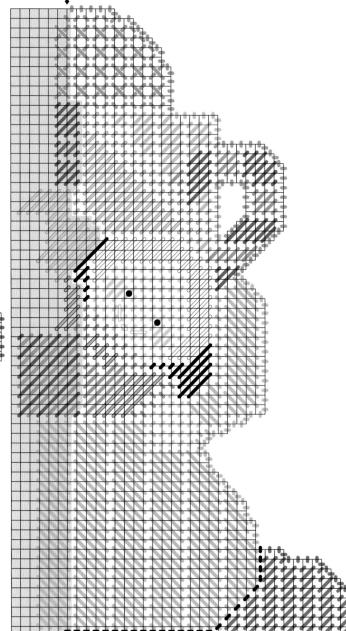

| COLOR | COLOR |
|---|---|
| white | lt green |
| dk gold | green |
| orange | beige |
| peach | black |
| lt pink | metallic gold |
| pink | ● black Fr. knot |
| red | |

**Section D (38 x 64 threads)**

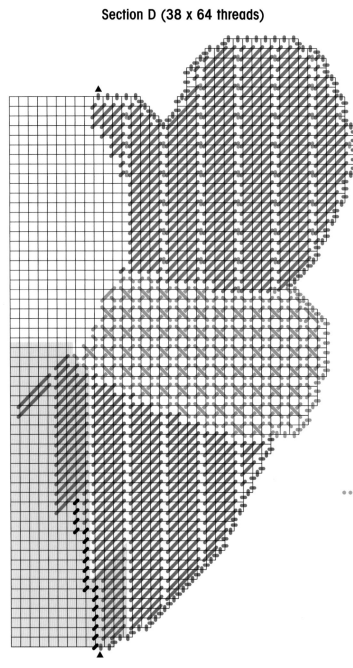

# GOODY BASKET BOUTIQUE

(Shown on page 19.)
**Skill Level:** Beginner
**Size:** 4³/₄"w x 5³/₄"h x 4³/₄"d
*(Fits a 4¹/₄"w x 5¹/₄"h x 4¹/₄"d boutique tissue box.)*

**Supplies:** Worsted weight yarn (refer to color key), two 10¹/₂" x 13¹/₂" sheets of clear 7 mesh plastic canvas, and #16 tapestry needle.

**Stitches Used:** Backstitch, Cross Stitch, French Knot, Overcast Stitch, Reversed Tent Stitch, and Tent Stitch.

**Instructions:** Follow charts to cut and stitch Tissue Box Cover pieces, working backstitches and French knots last. Referring to photo for yarn color, use overcast stitches to join Sides along long edges. Matching ▲'s, place Handles on opposite Sides. Join Top to Handles and Sides. Referring to photo, tack Brads to Handles and Sides.

**Handle (6 x 32 threads) (stitch 2)**

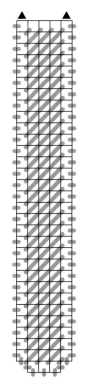

**Brad (3 x 3 threads) (stitch 2)**

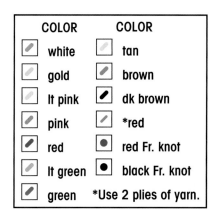

| COLOR | COLOR |
|---|---|
| white | tan |
| gold | brown |
| lt pink | dk brown |
| pink | *red |
| red | red Fr. knot |
| lt green | black Fr. knot |
| green | *Use 2 plies of yarn. |

**Side (32 x 38 threads) (stitch 4)**

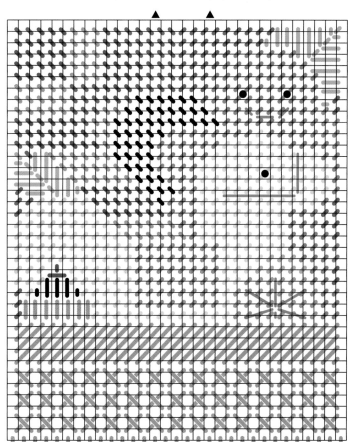

**Top (32 x 32 threads)**

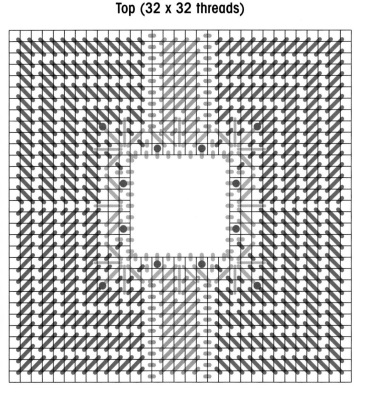

# GLORIOUS ANGEL

(Shown on page 20.)

**Skill Level:** Intermediate

**Size:** 9⅝"w x 12"h x 2½"d

**Supplies:** Worsted weight yarn (refer to color keys), four 10½" x 13½" sheets of clear 7 mesh plastic canvas, #16 tapestry needle, sewing needle and thread, ninety-six 3mm white pearl beads, and 15" length of ¼" dia. wooden dowel.

**Stitches Used:** Backstitch, French Knot, Gobelin Stitch, Overcast Stitch, and Tent Stitch.

**Instructions:** Follow charts to cut and stitch Angel pieces, working backstitches and French knots last and leaving pink shaded areas unworked. Using sewing needle and thread, attach beads to stitched pieces. Use white overcast stitches for all joining. Referring to Diagram, place dowel on wrong side of Angel Body Back. Stitch dowel to Angel Body Back. Matching ▲'s, place Right Wing on Left Wing. Work stitches in pink shaded areas to join Left Wing to Right Wing. Referring to photo, tack right side of Wings to right side of Angel Body Back. Matching ▼'s and ★'s, tack wrong side of Arms to wrong side of Angel Body Front. Referring to photo, tack Arms to right side of Angel Body Front. With wrong sides together, join Angel Body Front to Angel Body Back along side edges below ▼'s. Join Angel Body Front to Angel Body Back above ★'s. Referring to photo, tack Star to Arms.

**Angel Body Front (46 x 81 threads)**

| COLOR | |
|---|---|
| 🖊 | white |
| 🖊 | orange |
| 🖊 | peach |
| 🖊 | pink |
| 🖊 | lt brown |
| ● | black Fr. knot |
| ◉ | pearl bead placement |

**Diagram**

**Angel Body Back (46 x 81 threads)**

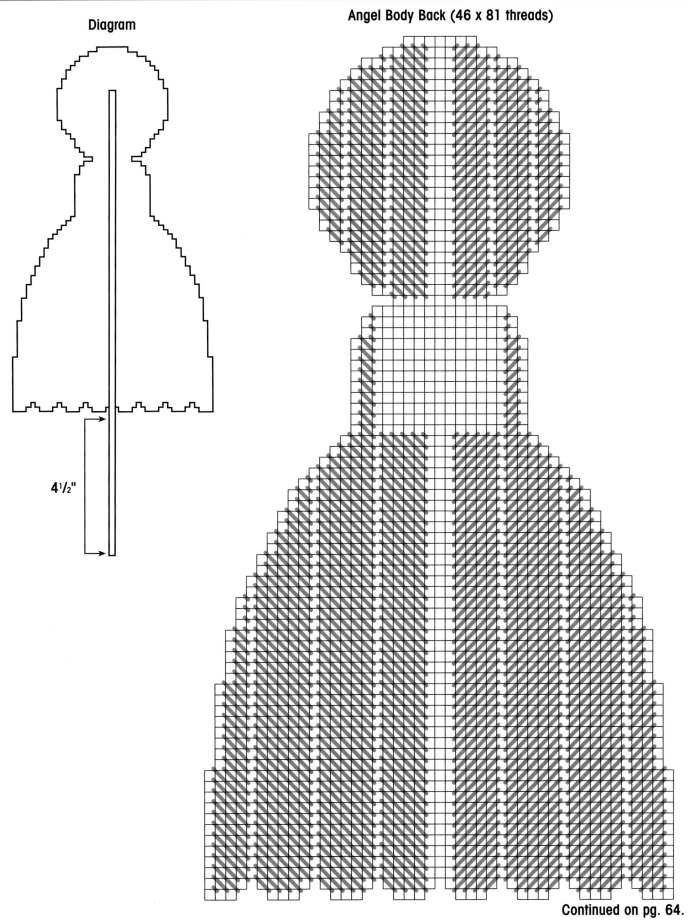

4¹/₂"

**Continued on pg. 64.**

63

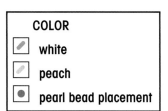

**Star (26 x 26 threads)**

**Arms (69 x 35 threads)**

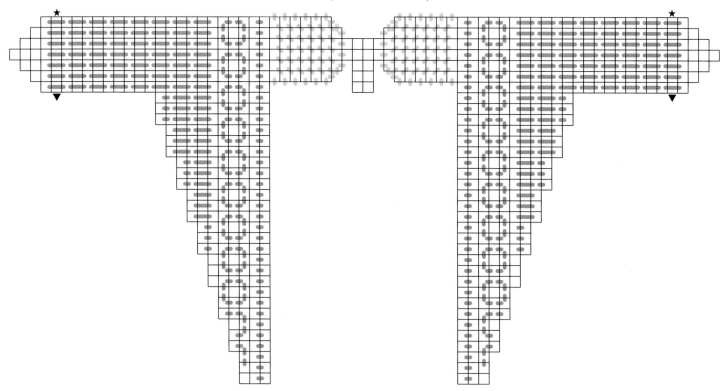

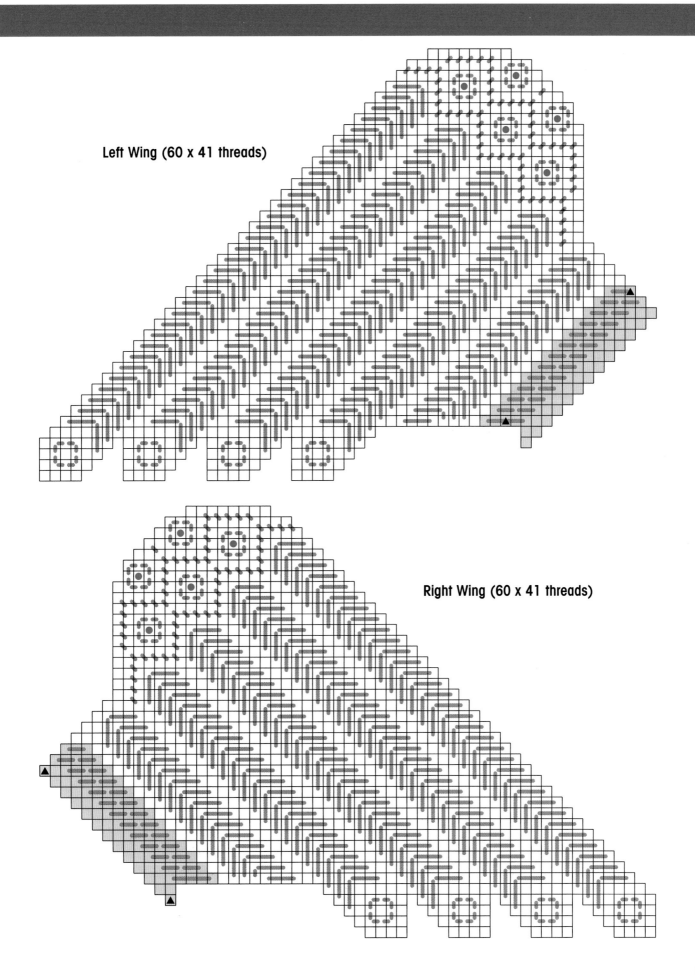

Left Wing (60 x 41 threads)

Right Wing (60 x 41 threads)

## ANGEL WITH HARP

(Shown on page 21.)

**Skill Level:** Beginner

**Size:** 6¼"w x 6¼"h

**Supplies:** Worsted weight yarn, metallic gold braid, and metallic gold embroidery floss (refer to color key); one 10½" x 13½" sheet of clear 7 mesh plastic canvas; #16 tapestry needle; thirteen 4mm gold beads; nylon thread and sewing needle; and craft glue.

**Stitches Used:** Backstitch, French Knot, Gobelin Stitch, Overcast Stitch, Tent Stitch, and Turkey Loop Stitch.

**Instructions:** Follow charts to cut and stitch Angel pieces, working backstitches, French knots, and Turkey loops last. Attach beads to Angel using nylon thread. For left ponytail, make a 2" braid using three lengths of brown yarn. Fold braid into two loops and glue ends to back of Face. Tie a 12" length of green yarn into a small bow around braid loops and trim ends. Repeat to make right ponytail. Tack Arm to Angel. Matching ▲'s, glue Face to Angel. Glue Harp to Angel. For hanger, thread 8" length of nylon thread through top of Angel. Knot ends of nylon thread 3" above Angel; trim ends.

| COLOR | |
|---|---|
| ✏ | white |
| ✏ | yellow |
| ✏ | flesh |
| ✏ | pink |
| ✏ | green |
| ✏ | brown |
| ✏ | metallic gold braid |
| ✏ | *metallic gold |
| ✏ | †dk pink |
| ● | †black Fr. knot |
| ○ | brown Turkey loop |
| ● | bead placement |

*Use 6 strands of floss.

†Use 2 plies of yarn.

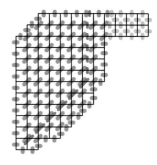

**Arm (13 x 13 threads)**

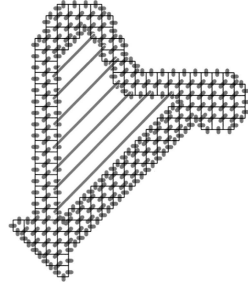

**Harp (22 x 25 threads)**

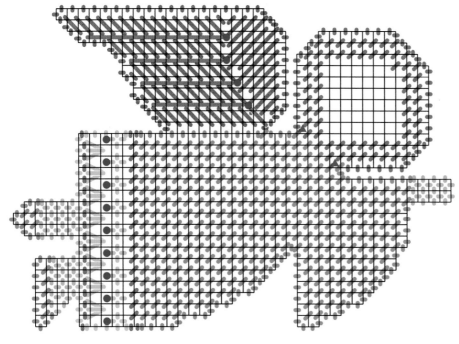

**Angel (41 x 29 threads)**

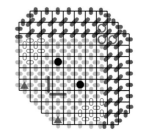

**Face (11 x 11 threads)**

## ANGEL WITH HORN

(Shown on page 21.)

**Skill Level:** Beginner

**Size:** 5¼"w x 6"h

**Supplies:** Worsted weight yarn and metallic gold braid (refer to color key), one 10½" x 13½" sheet of clear 7 mesh plastic canvas, #16 tapestry needle, thirty-five 4mm gold beads, nylon thread and sewing needle, 12" bamboo skewer, and craft glue.

**Stitches Used:** Alicia Lace Stitch, Backstitch, French Knot, Gobelin Stitch, Overcast Stitch, Scotch Stitch, and Tent Stitch.

**Instructions:** Follow charts to cut and stitch Angel pieces, working backstitches and French knots last and leaving stitches in pink shaded areas unworked. Attach beads to Angel using nylon thread. Wrap a one yard piece of tan yarn tightly around skewer to form a coil. Run a narrow bead of glue down coiled yarn. Allow glue to dry and remove coiled yarn from skewer. Cut coiled yarn into 1" ringlet pieces. Glue three ringlets to left side of Face. Tie a 6" length of lavender yarn in a knot around left ringlets and trim ends to ½" long. Separate plies of yarn on ends. Repeat for right side of Face. Glue two ringlets to top of Face. Matching ■'s, place Arms on top of Angel and work stitches in pink shaded areas to join Arms to Angel. Matching ▲'s, glue Face to Angel. Glue Horn to Angel. For hanger, thread 8" length of nylon thread through top of Angel. Knot ends of nylon thread 3" above Angel; trim ends.

| | COLOR |
|---|---|
| ✎ | white |
| ✎ | yellow |
| ✎ | flesh |
| ✐ | pink |
| ✎ | lavender |
| ✎ | tan |
| ✎ | metallic gold braid |
| ✎ | *dk pink |
| ● | yellow Fr. knot |
| ● | *black Fr. knot |
| ● | bead placement |

**\*Use 2 plies of yarn.**

**Arms (19 x 19 threads)**

**Horn (19 x 19 threads)**

**Angel (34 x 34 threads)**

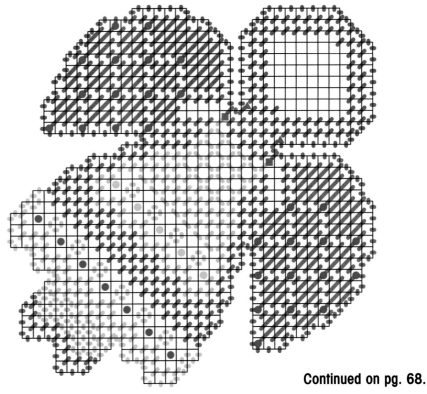

**Face (11 x 11 threads)**

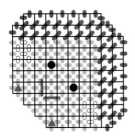

**Continued on pg. 68.**

## ANGEL WITH FLUTE

(Shown on page 21.)

**Skill Level:** Beginner

**Size:** 5½"w x 6¼"h

**Supplies:** Worsted weight yarn and metallic gold braid (refer to color key), one 10½" x 13½" sheet of clear 7 mesh plastic canvas, #16 tapestry needle, fifteen 4mm gold beads, nylon thread and sewing needle, and craft glue.

**Stitches Used:** Backstitch, French Knot, Gobelin Stitch, Overcast Stitch, Tent Stitch, and Turkey Loop Stitch.

**Instructions:** Follow charts to cut and stitch Angel pieces, working backstitches and French knots last and leaving stitches in blue shaded areas unworked. Attach beads to Angel using nylon thread. For left pigtail, tie a 12" length of pink yarn into a small bow around Turkey Loops and trim ends. Repeat for right pigtail. Matching ■'s, place Arms on top of Angel and work stitches in blue shaded areas to join Arms to Angel. Matching ▲'s, glue Face to Angel. Glue Flute to Angel. For hanger, thread 8" length of nylon thread through top of Angel. Knot ends of nylon thread 3" above Angel; trim ends.

| COLOR | |
|---|---|
| ✎ | white |
| ✎ | yellow |
| ✎ | flesh |
| ✎ | pink |
| ✎ | blue |
| ✎ | brown |
| ✎ | metallic gold braid |
| ✎ | *dk pink |
| ● | *black Fr. knot |
| ○ | yellow Turkey loop |
| ● | bead placement |

*Use 2 plies of yarn.

**Flute (2 x 18 threads)**

**Face (11 x 11 threads)**

**Angel (29 x 40 threads)**

**Arms (20 x 20 threads)**

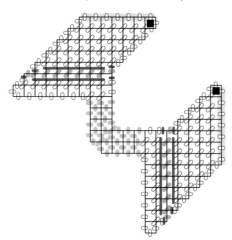

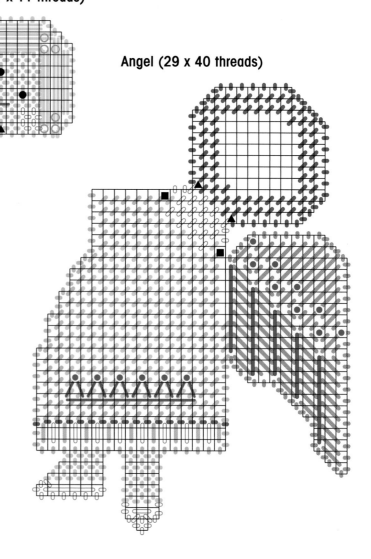

# CANDY CANE SANTAS

## TISSUE BOX COVER
(Shown on page 33.)
**Skill Level:** Beginner
**Size:** 4⁷/₈"w x 6⁵/₈"h x 4⁷/₈"d
*(Fits a 4¹/₄"w x 5¹/₄"h x 4¹/₄"d boutique tissue box.)*
**Supplies:** Worsted weight yarn (refer to color key), two
10¹/₂" x 13¹/₂" sheets of clear 7 mesh plastic canvas, and
#16 tapestry needle.
**Stitches Used:** Backstitch, French Knot, Gobelin Stitch, Overcast
Stitch, and Tent Stitch.

**Instructions:** Follow charts to cut and stitch Tissue Box Cover
pieces, working backstitches and French knots last. Use matching
color overcast stitches for all joining. Matching ★'s, join Back
pieces to Top. Matching ▲'s, join Sides to Back pieces. Join Sides
along long edges.

| COLOR | |
|---|---|
| ⟋ | white |
| ⟋ | peach |
| ⟋ | pink |
| ⟋ | red |
| ⟋ | green |
| ⟋ | *black |
| ◉ | *red Fr. Knot |
| *Use 2 plies of yarn. | |

**Back (32 x 7 threads) (stitch 4)**

**Side (32 x 44 threads) (stitch 4)**

**Top (32 x 32 threads)**

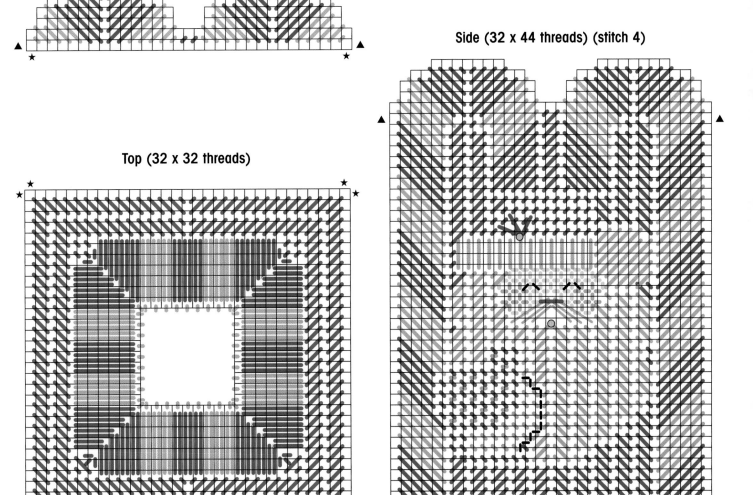

Continued on pg. 70.

## WREATH

(Shown on page 32.)

**Skill Level:** Beginner

**Santa Size:** 10"w x 10"h

**Supplies:** Worsted weight yarn (refer to color key), one 10½" x 13½" sheet of clear 7 mesh plastic canvas, #16 tapestry needle, wreath, additional decorations, and craft glue.

**Stitches Used:** Backstitch, Gobelin Stitch, Overcast Stitch, and Tent Stitch.

**Instructions:** Follow charts to cut and stitch Wreath pieces, working backstitches stitches last. Referring to photo, glue Holly and Snowflake to Santa. Glue Santa to Wreath. Add additional decorations to Wreath as desired.

## SLEIGH ORNAMENT

(Shown on page 33.)

**Skill Level:** Beginner

**Size:** 2¾"w x 3¼"h

**Supplies:** Sport weight yarn (refer to color key), one 10½" x 13½" sheet of clear 10 mesh plastic canvas, and #20 tapestry needle, and nylon thread and sewing needle.

**Stitches Used:** Backstitch, French Knot, Gobelin Stitch, Overcast Stitch, and Tent Stitch.

**Instructions:** Follow chart to cut and stitch Ornament, working backstitches and French knots last. For hanger, thread 8" length of nylon thread through top of Ornament. Knot ends of nylon thread 3" above Ornament; trim ends.

| COLOR | |
|---|---|
| ⬛ | white |
| ⬛ | peach |
| ⬛ | pink |
| ⬛ | red |
| ⬛ | green |
| ⬛ | black |
| ⬛ | metallic gold |
| ● | *red Fr. knot |
| ● | *black Fr. knot |

*Use 2 plies of yarn.

**Sleigh Ornament (32 x 31 threads)**

**Wreath Snowflake (14 x 14 threads)**

**Wreath Holly (12 x 9 threads)**

**Wreath Santa (67 x 67 threads)**

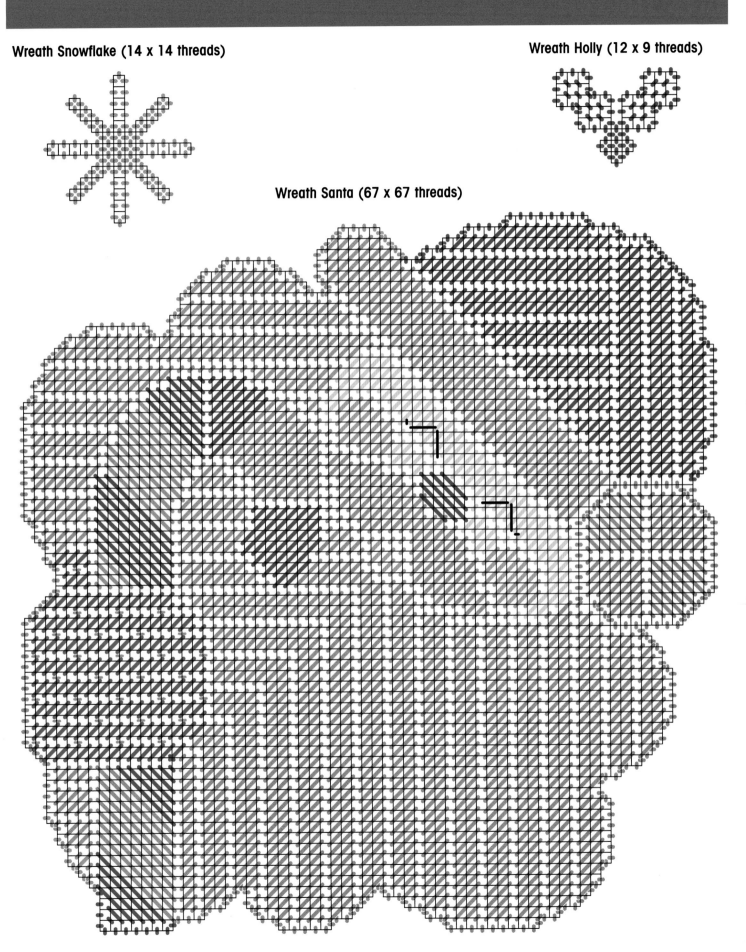

# DECK THE TREE

(Shown on pages 22-23.)

**Skill Level:** Beginner

**Approx. Size:** 4"w x 4³/₈"h each

**Supplies:** Worsted weight yarn and Rainbow Gallery metallic gold yarn (refer to color key), one 10¹/₂" x 13¹/₂" sheet of clear 7 mesh plastic canvas, #16 tapestry needle, nylon thread and sewing needle, and craft glue.

**Stitches Used:** Backstitch, Cross Stitch, French Knot, Fringe Stitch, Gobelin Stitch, Overcast Stitch, and Tent Stitch.

**Instructions:** Follow chart(s) to cut and stitch desired Ornament pieces, working backstitches, French knots, and fringe stitches last. For hanger, thread 8" length of nylon thread through top of Ornament. Knot ends of nylon thread 3″ above Ornament; trim ends. *For Snowman only,* referring to photo, glue Nose to Snowman. Referring to photo, glue Scarf End to back of Snowman.

**Nutcracker (20 x 40 threads)**

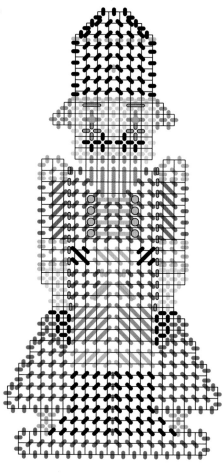

**Elf (30 x 29 threads)**

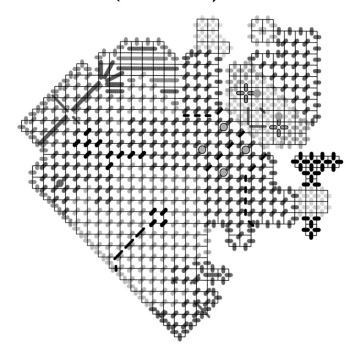

**Reindeer (26 x 26 threads)**

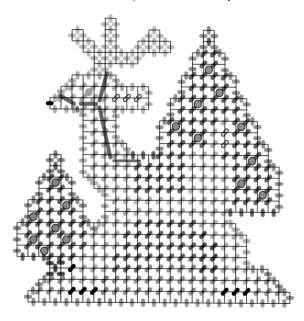

**Star (28 x 28 threads)**

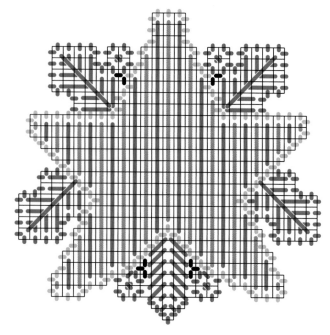

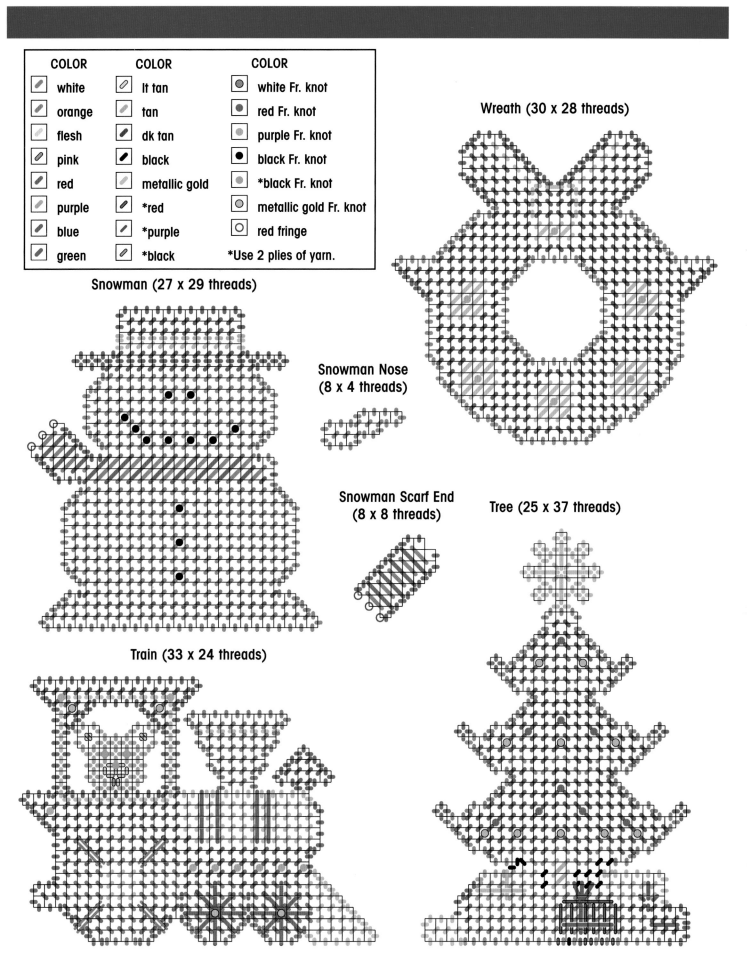

**COLOR**

| | | | |
|---|---|---|---|
| white | lt tan | white Fr. knot |
| orange | tan | red Fr. knot |
| flesh | dk tan | purple Fr. knot |
| pink | black | black Fr. knot |
| red | metallic gold | *black Fr. knot |
| purple | *red | metallic gold Fr. knot |
| blue | *purple | red fringe |
| green | *black | *Use 2 plies of yarn. |

Wreath (30 x 28 threads)

Snowman (27 x 29 threads)

Snowman Nose
(8 x 4 threads)

Snowman Scarf End
(8 x 8 threads)

Tree (25 x 37 threads)

Train (33 x 24 threads)

## DOORSTOP

(Shown on page 25.)

**Skill Level:** Beginner

**Size:** 6¼"w x 11"h x 2½"d

*(Holds a 3⅝"w x 8"h x 2⅛"d brick.)*

**Supplies:** Worsted weight yarn (refer to color key), two 10½" x 13½" sheets of clear 7 mesh plastic canvas, #16 tapestry needle, brick, plastic wrap, and craft glue.

**Stitches Used:** Backstitch, Cross Stitch, French Knot, Gobelin Stitch, Overcast Stitch, and Tent Stitch.

**Instructions:** Follow charts to cut and stitch Doorstop pieces, working backstitches and French knots last. Using green overcast stitches, join Long Sides to Short Sides along short edges. Join Sides to Front. Wrap brick in plastic wrap. Place brick inside Doorstop. Join Back to Sides. Referring to photo, glue Santa to Front.

**Short Side (27 x 17 threads) (stitch 2)**

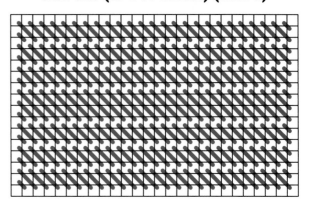

**Front/Back (27 x 56 threads) (stitch 2)**

**Long Side (17 x 56 threads) (stitch 2)**

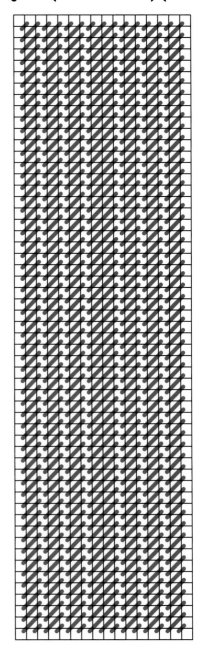

**Santa (42 x 74 threads)**

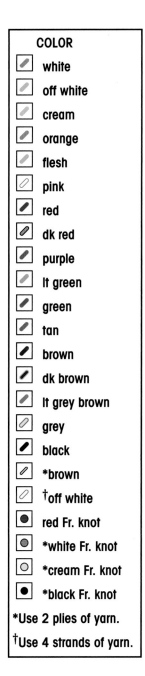

COLOR
| | |
|---|---|
| | white |
| | off white |
| | cream |
| | orange |
| | flesh |
| | pink |
| | red |
| | dk red |
| | purple |
| | lt green |
| | green |
| | tan |
| | brown |
| | dk brown |
| | lt grey brown |
| | grey |
| | black |
| | *brown |
| | †off white |
| ● | red Fr. knot |
| ● | *white Fr. knot |
| ○ | *cream Fr. knot |
| ● | *black Fr. knot |

*Use 2 plies of yarn.

†Use 4 strands of yarn.

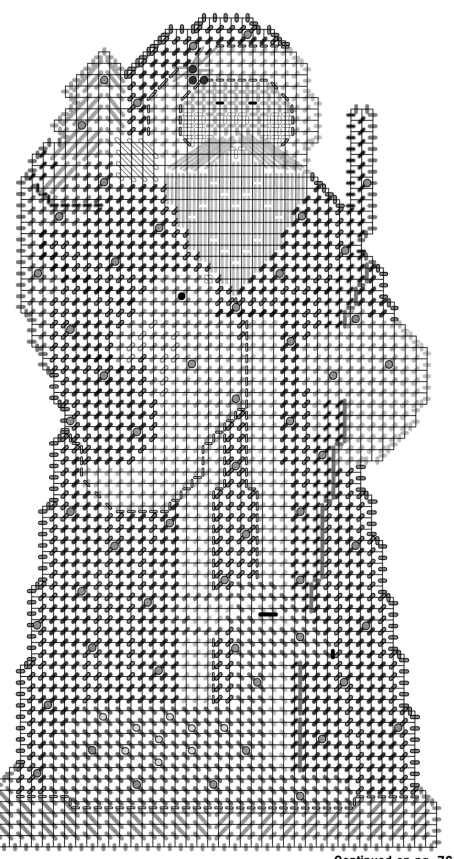

**Continued on pg. 76.**

## CENTERPIECE

(Shown on page 24.)

**Skill Level:** Intermediate

**Size:** 8³/₄"w x 10⁵/₈"h x 3¹/₂"d

**Supplies:** Worsted weight yarn (refer to color keys), six 10¹/₂" x 13¹/₂" sheets of clear 7 mesh plastic canvas, #16 tapestry needle, and craft glue.

**Stitches Used:** Backstitch, Cross Stitch, French Knot, Fringe Stitch, Gobelin Stitch, Overcast Stitch, Tent Stitch, and Turkey Loop Stitch.

**Instructions:** Follow charts to cut and stitch Centerpiece pieces, working backstitches, French knots, Turkey loops, and fringe stitches last and leaving blue shaded area unworked. Matching ▲'s, work stitches in blue shaded area to join Arm to Front. Unless otherwise indicated, use matching color overcast stitches for remainder of joining. For each Tree Center, join one Tree Center A to one Tree Center B. Referring to photo, tack Tree Center to Tree Back. Join Standing Deer Side A to Standing Deer Side B along unworked edges. Matching ■'s and ★'s, tack Standing Deer to Standing Deer Base. Join Reclining Deer Side A to Reclining Deer Side B along unworked edges. Matching ♦'s and ✖'s, tack Reclining Deer to Reclining Deer Base. For Santa Back, cut a piece of plastic canvas 58 x 19 threads. Santa Back is not worked. Align short ends of Santa Back with short ends of Santa Front, keeping one long edge of Santa Back even with bottom edge of Santa Front. Join short ends of Santa Back to wrong side of Santa Front. Using matching color overcast stitches, cover remaining unworked edges. Referring to photo, glue Squirrel, Bluebird, Skunk, Fox, and Bear to Centerpiece.

| COLOR | | COLOR | |
|---|---|---|---|
| ⊘ | white | ⊘ | taupe |
| ⊘ | off white | ⊘ | brown |
| ⊘ | cream | ⊘ | dk brown |
| ⊘ | dk orange | ⊘ | lt grey brown |
| ⊘ | flesh | ⊘ | black |
| ⊘ | pink | ⊘ | *brown |
| ⊘ | red | ⊘ | *lt grey brown |
| ⊘ | dk red | ⊙ | *white Fr. knot |
| ⊘ | lt blue | ⊙ | *cream Fr. knot |
| ⊘ | blue | ⊙ | *pink Fr. knot |
| ⊘ | lt green | ⬤ | *red Fr. knot |
| ⊘ | green | ⊙ | *lt tan Fr. knot |
| ⊘ | rust | ⬤ | *black Fr. Knot |
| ⊘ | lt tan | ◎ | lt green Turkey loop |
| ⊘ | tan | ◎ | lt green fringe |
| ⊘ | dk tan | | *Use 2 plies of yarn. |

### Squirrel (14 x 13 threads)

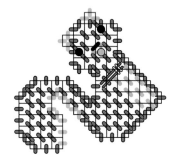

### Bluebird (9 x 10 threads)

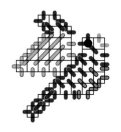

### Arm (14 x 13 threads)

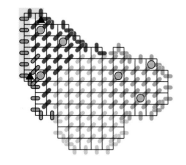

### Fox (23 x 15 threads)

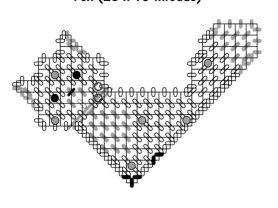

### Skunk (15 x 17 threads)

### Bear (17 x 15 threads)

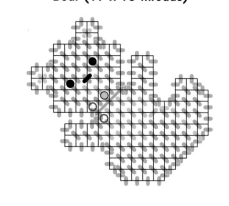

**Standing Deer Side A (30 x 36 threads)**

**Standing Deer Side B (30 x 36 threads)**

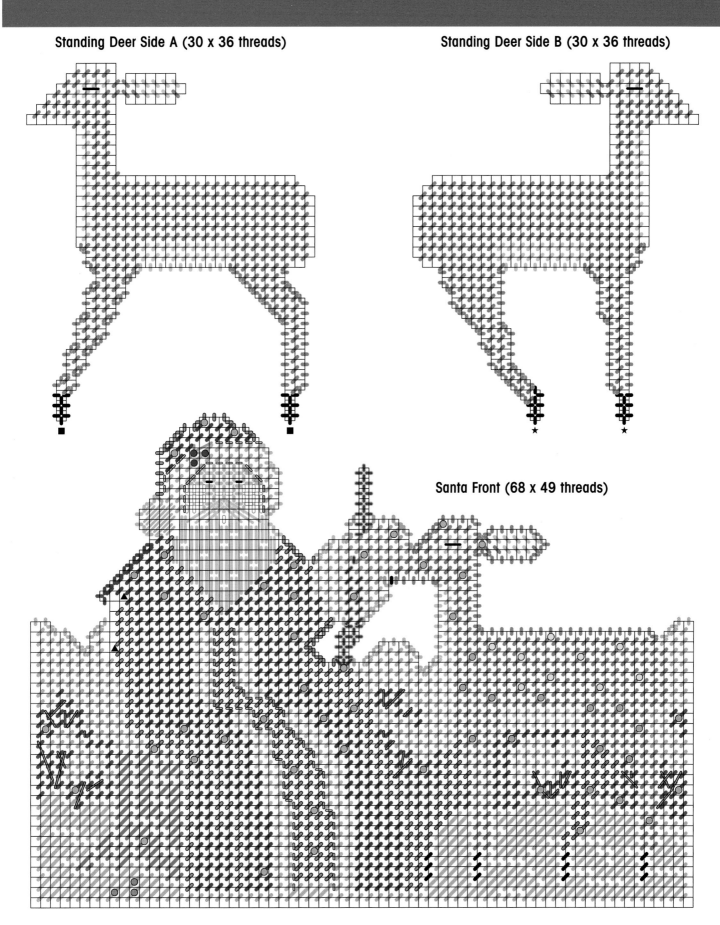

**Santa Front (68 x 49 threads)**

**Continued on pg. 78.**

**Tree Back**
**(44 x 71 threads) (stitch 2)**

**Reclining Deer Side A**
**(28 x 21 threads)**

**Reclining Deer Side B**
**(28 x 21 threads)**

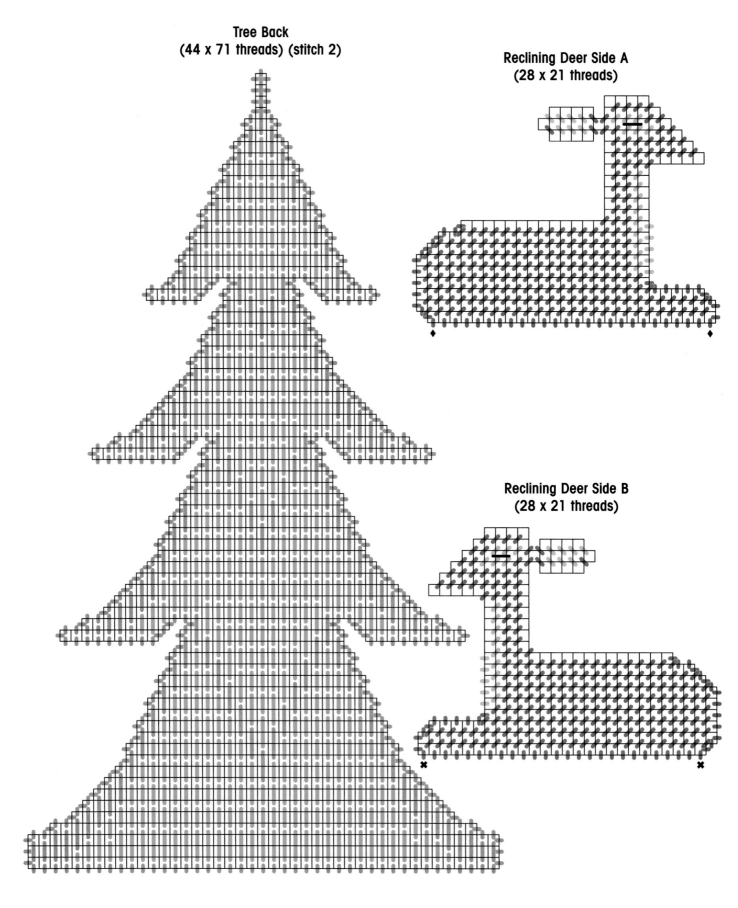

**Reclining Deer Base (35 x 15 threads)**

**Tree Center A**
**(23 x 71 threads) (stitch 2)**

**Tree Center B**
**(23 x 71 threads) (stitch 2)**

**Standing Deer Base (34 x 12 threads)**

**COLOR**
- ⊘ white
- ⊘ cream
- ⊘ lt green
- ⊘ tan
- ⊘ black

**Continued on pg. 80.**

## MAGNETS

(Shown on pages 24-25.)

**Skill Level:** Beginner

**Approx. Size:** 3¼"w x 3⅛"h each

**Supplies:** Worsted weight yarn (refer to color key), one 10½" x 13½" sheet of clear 7 mesh plastic canvas, #16 tapestry needle, magnetic strip, and craft glue.

**Stitches Used:** Backstitch, Cross Stitch, French Knot, Fringe Stitch, Gobelin Stitch, Overcast Stitch, Tent Stitch, and Turkey Loop Stitch.

**Instructions:** Follow chart to cut and stitch desired Magnet, working backstitches, French knots, Turkey loops, and fringe stitches last. Glue magnetic strip to back of Magnet.

| COLOR | COLOR |
|---|---|
| white | grey brown |
| off white | black |
| cream | *brown |
| flesh | *black |
| pink | *white Fr. knot |
| red | *pink Fr. knot |
| dk red | *red Fr. knot |
| lt green | *black Fr. knot |
| lt tan | lt green Turkey loop |
| brown | lt green fringe |
| lt grey brown | *Use 2 plies of yarn. |

**Raccoon (26 x 24 threads)**

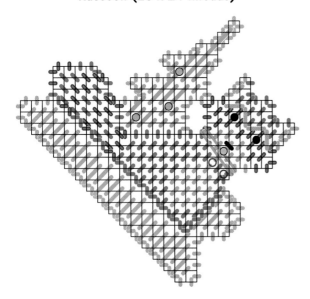

**Bear (23 x 25 threads)**

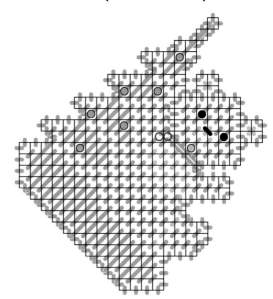

**Skunk (23 x 26 threads)**

**Santa (22 x 21 threads)**

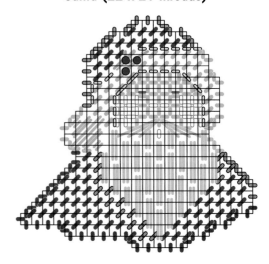

# HO-HO-HO TISSUE BOX

(Shown on page 28.)
**Skill Level:** Beginner
**Size:** $4^7/_8$"w x 7"h x $4^7/_8$"d
*(Fits a $4^1/_4$"w x $5^1/_4$"h x $4^1/_4$"d boutique tissue box.)*
**Supplies:** Worsted weight yarn and Rainbow Gallery metallic gold yarn (refer to color key), two $10^1/_2$" x $13^1/_2$" sheets of clear 7 mesh plastic canvas, and #16 tapestry needle.
**Stitches Used:** Backstitch, French Knot, Gobelin Stitch, Overcast Stitch, Tent Stitch, and Upright Cross Stitch.
**Instructions:** Follow charts to cut and stitch Tissue Box Cover pieces, working backstitches and French knots last. Using white overcast stitches, join Chimney pieces along short edges. Matching ▲'s, use white overcast stitches to join Chimney to Top. Using green overcast stitches, join Sides along long edges. Using white overcast stitches, join Top to Sides.

| COLOR | |
|---|---|
| ✎ | white |
| ✎ | red |
| ✎ | green |
| ✎ | brown |
| ✎ | metallic gold |
| ⦿ | red Fr. knot |

**Chimney (12 x 9 threads) (stitch 4)**

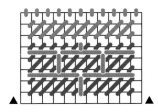

**Top (32 x 32 threads)**

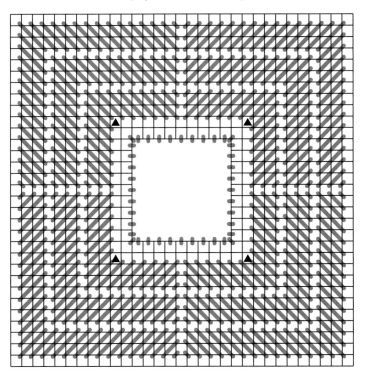

**Side (32 x 38 threads) (stitch 4)**

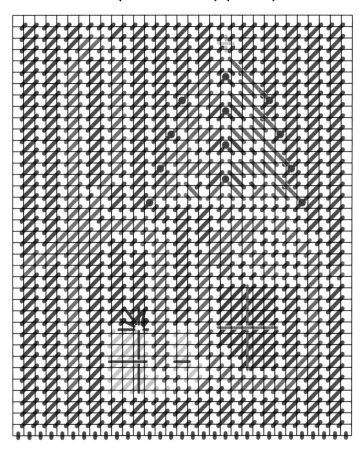

81

# MERRY SANTA

(Shown on page 26.)

**Skill Level:** Intermediate

**Size:** 10¼"w x 16½"h x 1¼"d

Supplies: Worsted weight yarn (refer to color key), three 10½" x 13½" sheets of clear 7 mesh plastic canvas, #16 tapestry needle, 15½" length of ¼" dia. wooden dowel, and tissue paper.

**Stitches Used:** Backstitch, Cross Stitch, French Knot, Gobelin Stitch, Overcast Stitch, and Tent Stitch.

**Instructions:** Follow charts to cut and stitch Santa pieces, working backstitches and French knots last. Back is not worked. Referring to Diagram, place dowel on Back. Using white overcast stitches, join dowel to Back. Using matching color overcast stitches, join Face to Front between ✖'s. Place Front and Back together with dowel between pieces. Using white overcast stitches and working through three thicknesses, join sides of Face to Front and Back between ▲'s. Matching ♥'s, place Arm A on Front and Back. Matching ■'s, place Arm B on Front and Back. Using matching color overcast stitches, join Front to Back, joining Arms in place and leaving areas between ★'s open. Use tissue paper to lightly stuff Santa. Using matching color overcast stitches, join Front to Back between ★'s. Referring to photo, tack Candy Cane to Arm A and Front.

**Diagram**

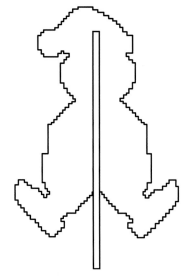

**Candy Cane (14 x 30 threads)**

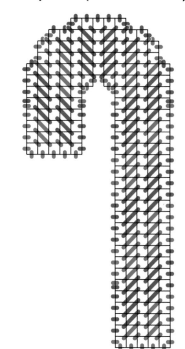

**Face (28 x 19 threads)**

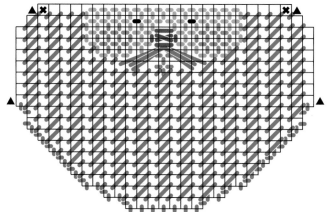

**Arm A (22 x 22 threads)**

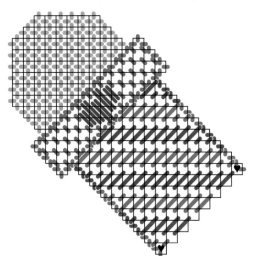

**Arm B (22 x 22 threads)**

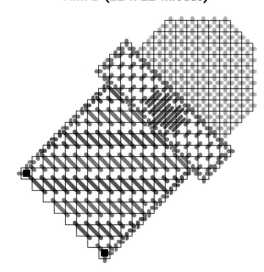

Front/Back (58 x 79 threads)
(cut 2) (stitch 1)

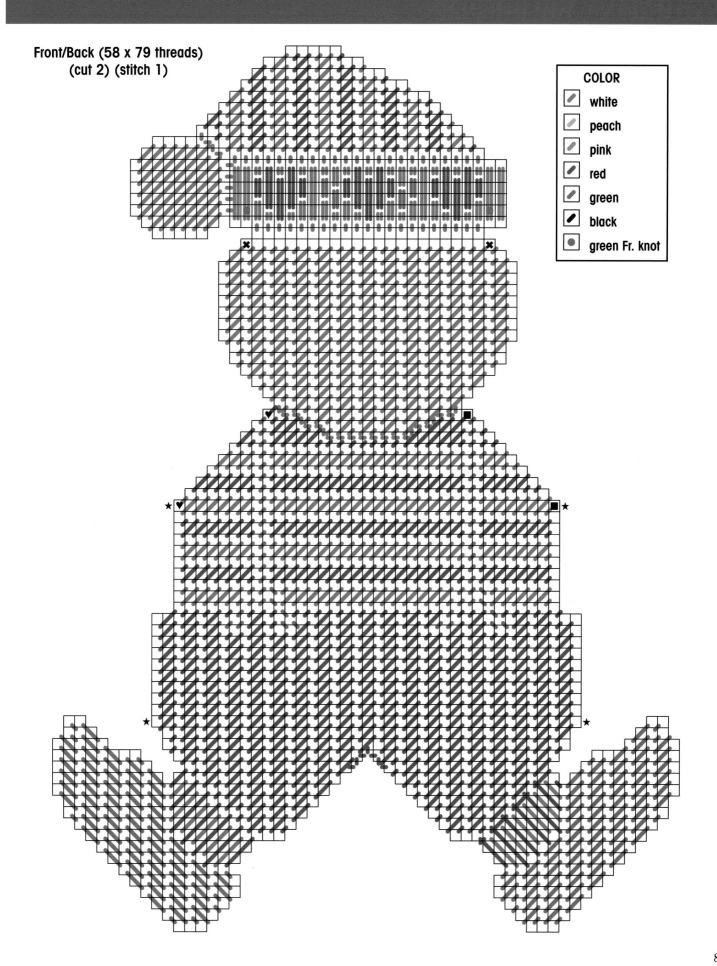

COLOR

| | |
|---|---|
| ✏ | white |
| ✏ | peach |
| ✏ | pink |
| ✏ | red |
| ✏ | green |
| ✏ | black |
| ● | green Fr. knot |

# SNOWMAN CARD HOLDER

(Shown on page 27.)
**Skill Level:** Advanced
**Size:** 14½"w x 14"h x 5½"d
**Supplies:** Worsted weight yarn or Needloft® Plastic Canvas Yarn (refer to color keys), four 10½" x 13½" sheets of white 7 mesh plastic canvas, #16 tapestry needle, three 2" white pom-poms, two 1½" white pom-poms, six 1" white pom-poms, one 12" length of ¼" dia. wooden dowel, and craft glue.
**Stitches Used:** Backstitch, French Knot, Fringe Stitch, Gobelin Stitch, Mosaic Stitch, Overcast Stitch, and Tent Stitch.
**Instructions:** You'll need to refer to the photo as you assemble your Card Holder. Follow charts to cut and stitch Card Holder pieces, working fringe stitches last and leaving green shaded area unworked. Holding wooden dowel on wrong side of Snowman, work stitches in green shaded area to join dowel to Snowman. Referring to Diagram, use white overcast stitches to join long edge of Fence Side A to one corresponding side edge of Fence Front. Repeat to join Fence Side B to Fence Front. Matching ★'s and ✖'s, use white overcast stitches to join Inside Fence Post to Fence Side A and Fence Front. Cut a piece of canvas 12 x 22 threads for Mailbox Bottom. Mailbox Bottom is not worked. Tack Mailbox Bottom to Inside Fence Post, Fence Side A, and Fence Front. Use white overcast stitches to join Mailbox Flap to short edge of Mailbox Bottom. Using white overcast stitches, join short edges of Mailbox Top to long edges of Mailbox Bottom. Using red French knot, join Mailbox Flag to Mailbox Top at ♣. Using white overcast stitches, join Mailbox Back to unworked edges of Mailbox Top and Mailbox Bottom. Tack Snowman Nose to Snowman. Matching ♦'s, use white overcast stitches to join Snowman Scarf to Snowman. Matching ▲'s and ■'s, use white overcast stitches to join Snowman to Fence Side A and Fence Side B. Using white overcast stitches, join Bottom to Snowman and Fence. Matching ♥'s, use red overcast stitches to join Redbird Wing to Redbird. Tack Redbird to Fence. Glue 2" and 1" pom-poms to Snowman. Glue 1½" pom-poms to Snowman at ▼'s. Trim Fringe on Snowman to 1" long. Using white overcast stitches, join Package Sides along long edges. Using matching color overcast stitches, join Package Top to Package Sides. Using white overcast stitches, join remaining unworked edges of Package to unworked area of Package Holder. Tie a 6" length of red yarn in a bow and trim ends. Glue bow to Package Top. Slide Package Holder into Mailbox.

**Package Top**
**(6 x 6 threads)**

**Package Side**
**(6 x 9 threads)**
**(stitch 4)**

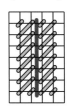

**Package Holder**
**(11 x 21 threads)**

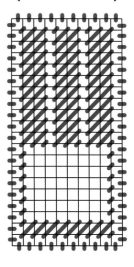

**Redbird (22 x 22 threads)**

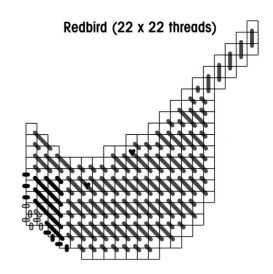

**Diagram**

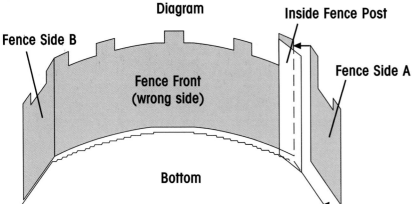

Fence Side B

Inside Fence Post

Fence Front
(wrong side)

Fence Side A

Bottom

**Redbird Wing (14 x 8 threads)**

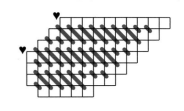

84

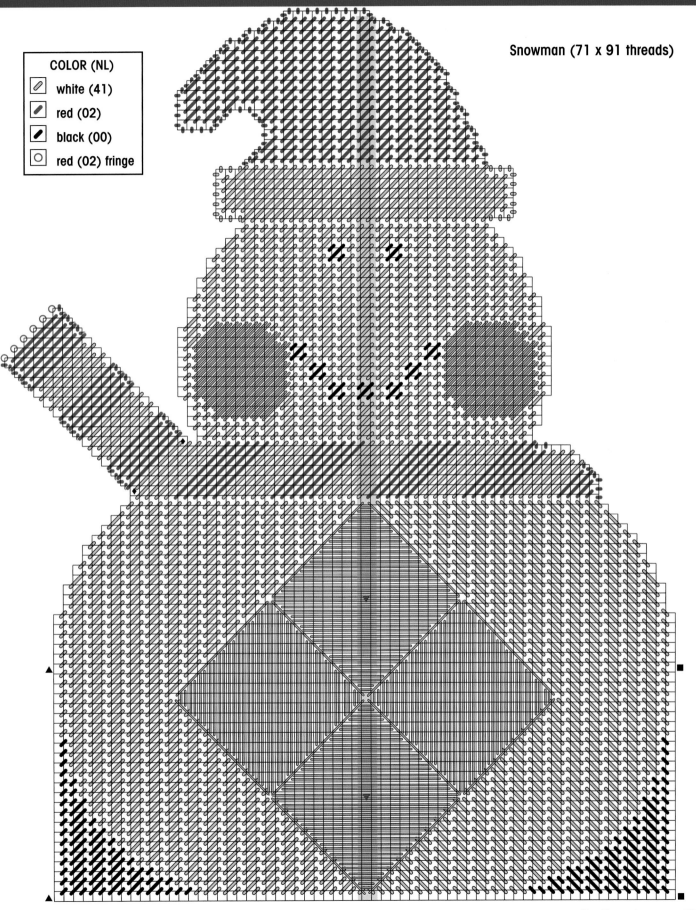

**Snowman (71 x 91 threads)**

**Continued on pg. 86.**

COLOR (NL)

white (41)

red (02)

black (00)

red (02) fringe

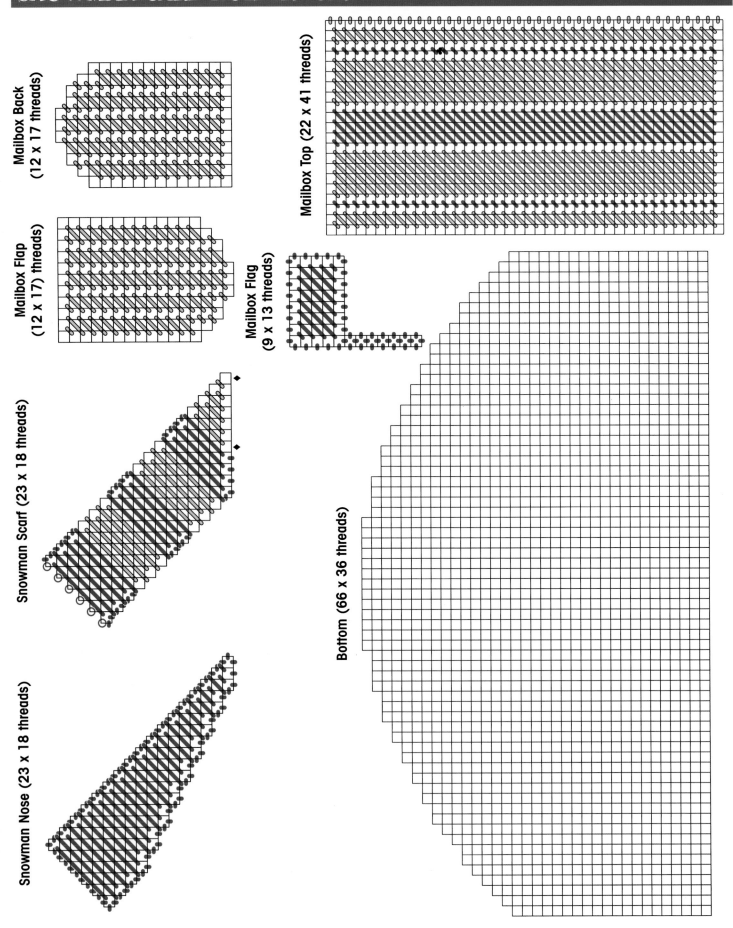

Mailbox Back
(12 x 17 threads)

Mailbox Top (22 x 41 threads)

Mailbox Flap
(12 x 17) threads)

Mailbox Flag
(9 x 13 threads)

Snowman Scarf (23 x 18 threads)

Snowman Nose (23 x 18 threads)

Bottom (66 x 36 threads)

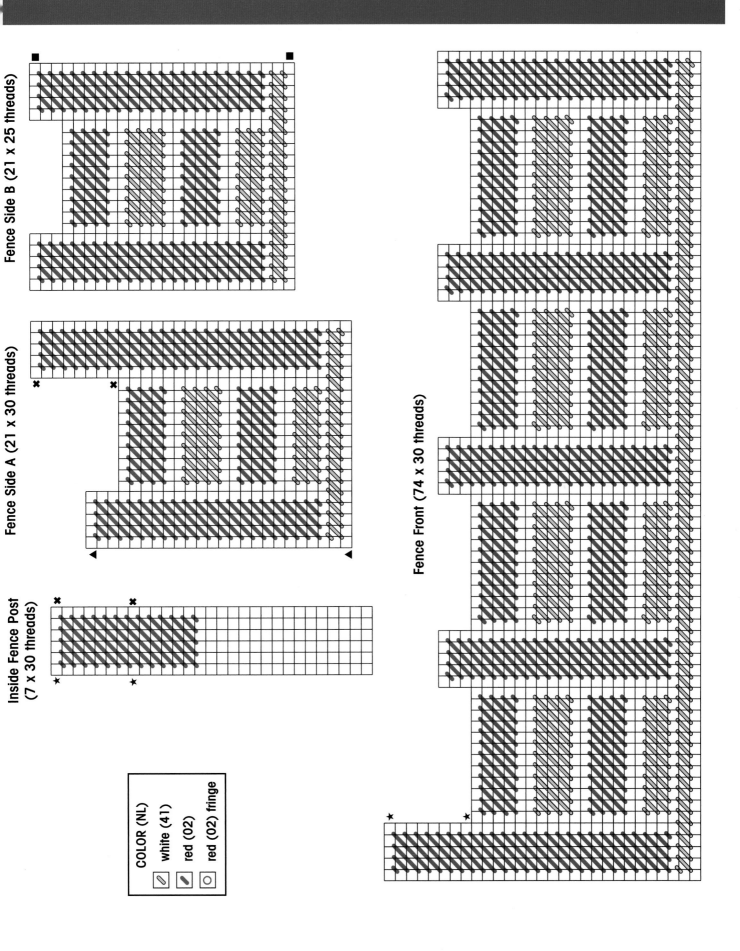

Fence Side B (21 x 25 threads)

Fence Side A (21 x 30 threads)

Inside Fence Post
(7 x 30 threads)

Fence Front (74 x 30 threads)

COLOR (NL)

white (41)

red (02)

red (02) fringe

# SNOWMAN CANISTER

**Head Front (26 x 33 threads)**

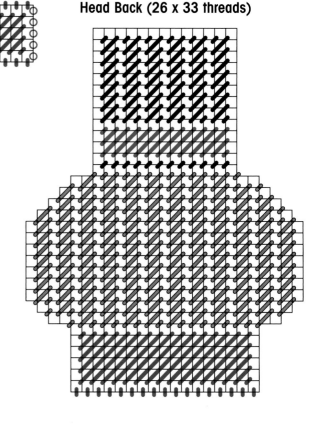

(Shown on page 30.)
**Skill Level:** Advanced
**Size:** 6¹/₂"w x 8¹/₂"h x 3⁵/₈"d
**Supplies:** Worsted weight yarn (refer to color key), two 10¹/₂" x 13¹/₂" sheets of clear 7 mesh plastic canvas, and #16 tapestry needle.
**Stitches Used:** Fringe Stitch, Gobelin Stitch, Overcast Stitch, and Tent Stitch.
**Instructions:** Follow charts to cut and stitch Canister pieces, working fringe stitches last. Matching ▲'s, use black overcast stitches to join Hat Sides to Hat Top. Matching ✖'s, use black overcast stitches to join Head Sides to Hat Sides. Matching ♥'s, use red overcast stitches to join Scarf Sides to Head Sides. Using matching color overcast stitches, join Scarf Sides, Head Sides, Hat Sides, and Hat Top to Head Front and Head Back. Slide Hat Brim onto Hat; tack Hat Brim in place. Matching ♦'s, use white overcast stitches to join Body Sides to Bottom. Using matching color overcast stitches, join Body Sides and Bottom to Body Front and Body Back. Referring to photo, tack Scarf End A and Scarf End B to Body Side.

| COLOR | |
|---|---|
| 🖊 | white |
| 🖊 | red |
| 🖊 | green |
| 🖊 | black |
| ◎ | red fringe |

**Scarf Side**
**(14 x 7 threads) (stitch 2)**

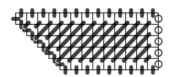

**Scarf End A (14 x 6 threads)**

**Scarf End B (15 x 6 threads)**

**Head Back (26 x 33 threads)**

**Hat Brim (30 x 24 threads)**

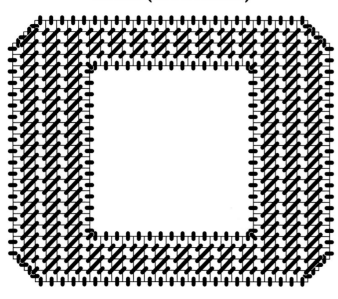

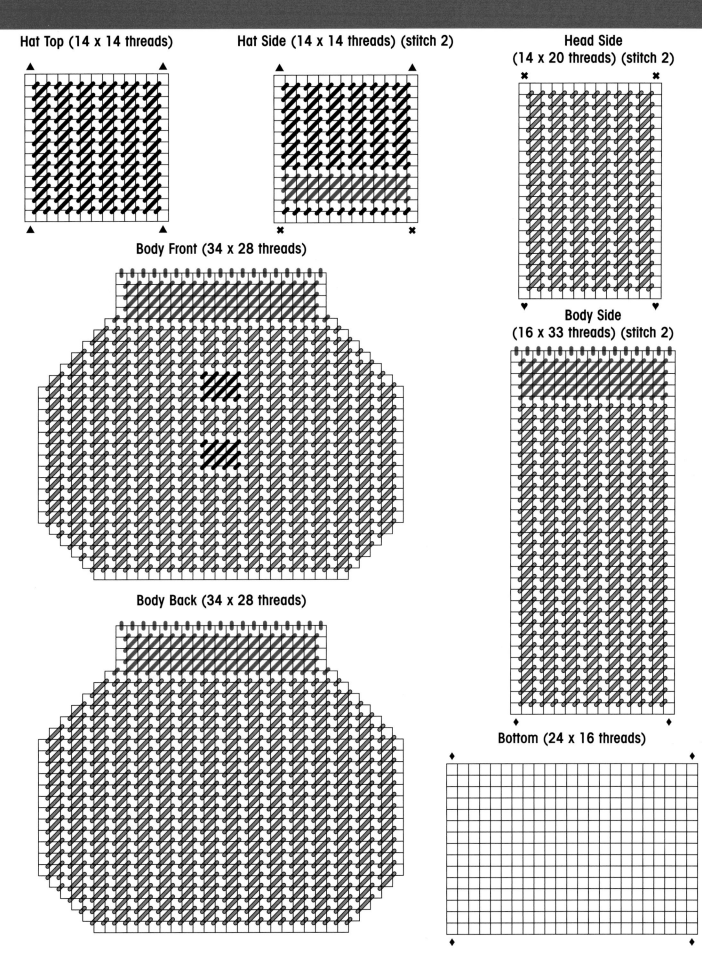

Hat Top (14 x 14 threads)

Hat Side (14 x 14 threads) (stitch 2)

Head Side
(14 x 20 threads) (stitch 2)

Body Front (34 x 28 threads)

Body Side
(16 x 33 threads) (stitch 2)

Body Back (34 x 28 threads)

Bottom (24 x 16 threads)

# TREETOP ANGEL BEAR

(Shown on page 29.)
**Skill Level:** Intermediate
**Size:** 10"w x 10½"h x 1¼"d
**Supplies:** Worsted weight yarn (refer to color key), two 10½" x 13½" sheets of clear 7 mesh plastic canvas, #16 tapestry needle, 2⅞ yds of ¼"w white ribbon, 12" length of ⅛" dia. wooden dowel, six 10" lengths of #26 gauge wire, and craft glue.
**Stitches Used:** Backstitch, French Knot, Gobelin Stitch, Overcast Stitch, and Tent Stitch.
**Instructions:** Follow charts to cut and stitch Tree Topper pieces, working backstitches and French knots last and leaving blue shaded area unworked. Turn Body over and work stitches in blue shaded area. With right side of head up, place dowel between ✖'s, with 5" of dowel extending below Body. Tack to secure dowel between ✖'s. Referring to photo, tack Holly to Head. Cut a 10" length of ribbon and tie in a bow. Glue bow to Head Front. With right sides up, tack Nose to Head Front. With wrong sides together and matching ▲'s and ♥'s, use tan overcast stitches to join Head Front to Body along unworked threads of Head Front. With wrong sides together and matching ■'s and ▼'s, use white overcast stitches to join Dress to Body between ■'s and ▼'s. With right sides up and matching ◗'s and ♣'s, use white overcast stitches to join Arms to body between ◗'s and ♣'s. Cut three 30" lengths of ribbon. Fold each length in half. Place folded ends together. Referring to photo, glue folded ends to wrong side of Arms. Glue Stars to ribbons; trim ends. Thread a 10" length of wire around dowel along each placement thread on Body. Wrap wire ends around tree. Use remaining 10" lengths of wire to attach lower portion of dowel to tree.

**Arms (30 x 30 threads)**

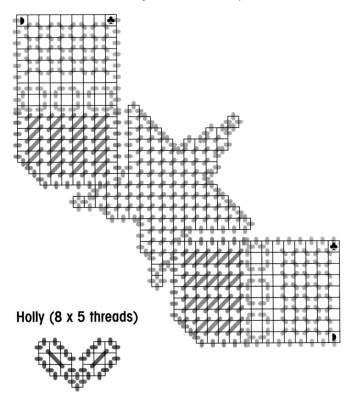

**Holly (8 x 5 threads)**

**Dress (32 x 32 threads)**

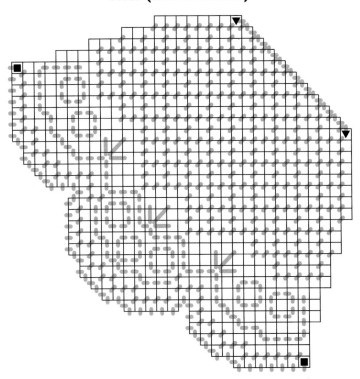

**Head Front (32 x 32 threads)**

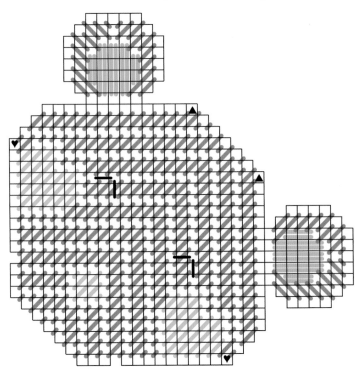

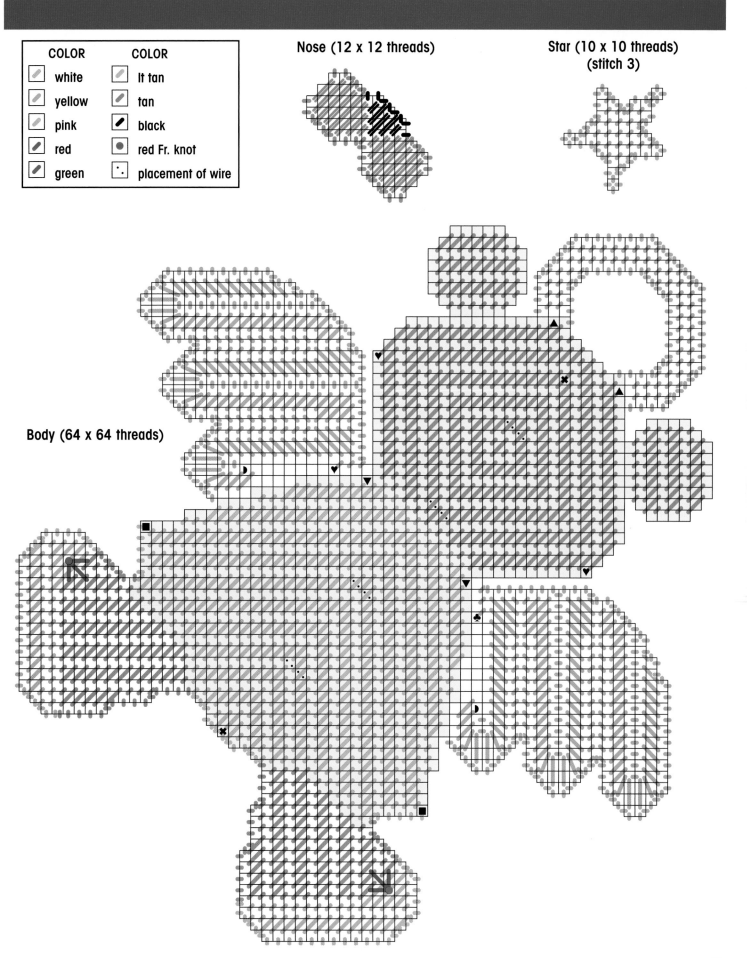

COLOR
- white
- yellow
- pink
- red
- green

COLOR
- lt tan
- tan
- black
- red Fr. knot
- placement of wire

Nose (12 x 12 threads)

Star (10 x 10 threads)
(stitch 3)

Body (64 x 64 threads)

# GENERAL INSTRUCTIONS

## SELECTING PLASTIC CANVAS

Plastic canvas is a molded material that consists of "threads" and "holes," but the threads aren't actually "threads" since the canvas is not woven. Project instructions often refer to the threads, especially when cutting out plastic canvas pieces. The holes are the spaces between the threads. The Stitch Diagrams, pages 94-96, will refer to holes when explaining where to place your needle to make a stitch.

## TYPES OF CANVAS

The main difference between types of plastic canvas is the mesh size. Mesh size refers to the number of holes in one inch of canvas. The projects in this book were stitched using 7 mesh and 10 mesh canvas. Seven mesh canvas is the most popular size.

7 mesh = 7 holes per inch
10 mesh = 10 holes per inch

Your project supply list will tell you the size mesh needed for your project. If your project calls for 7 mesh canvas and you use 10 mesh, your finished project will be much smaller than expected.

Most plastic canvas is clear, but colored plastic canvas is also available. Colored canvas is ideal when you don't want to stitch the entire background.

## AMOUNT OF CANVAS

The project supply list will tell you how much canvas will be needed to complete the project. As a general rule, it is better to buy too much canvas and have leftovers than to run out of canvas before you finish your project.

## SELECTING NEEDLES

### TYPES OF NEEDLES

A blunt needle called a tapestry needle is used for stitching on plastic canvas. Tapestry needles are sized by numbers; the higher the number, the smaller the needle. The correct size needle to use depends on the canvas mesh size and the yarn thickness. The needle should be small enough to allow the threaded needle to pass through the canvas holes easily. The eye of the needle should be large enough to allow yarn to be threaded easily. If the eye is too small, the yarn will wear thin and may break. You will find the recommended needle size listed in the supply section of each project. The chart below will be helpful if you need to select the correct needle for your project.

| Mesh | Needle |
|------|--------------|
| 7 | #16 tapestry |
| 10 | #20 tapestry |
| 14 | #24 tapestry |

## SELECTING YARN

We have a few hints to help you choose the perfect yarns for your project.

### COLORS

Your project will tell you what yarn colors you will need. Brand names and color numbers listed in some color keys are included only as a guide when choosing colors for your project. Choose colors and brands to suit your needs and your taste.

## TYPES OF YARN

The types of yarns available are endless, and each grouping of yarn has its own characteristics and uses. The following is a brief description of the yarns used for the projects in this book.

**Worsted Weight Yarn** - This yarn may be found in acrylic, wool, wool blends, and a variety of other fiber contents. Worsted weight yarn is the most popular yarn used for 7 mesh plastic canvas because one strand covers the canvas very well. This yarn is inexpensive and comes in a wide range of colors. Worsted weight yarn has four plies that are twisted together to form one strand. When the instructions call for two plies of yarn, you will need to separate a strand of yarn and use only two of the four plies.

**Needloft® Plastic Canvas Yarn** - This yarn is a 100% nylon worsted weight yarn and is suitable only for 7 mesh canvas. It will not easily separate. When stitching with Needloft and the instructions indicate two plies of yarn, substitute six strands of embroidery floss.

**Sport Weight Yarn** - Sport weight yarn works nicely for 10 mesh canvas. This yarn has three or four thin plies that are twisted together to form one strand. Like worsted weight yarn, sport weight yarn comes in a variety of fiber contents. The color selection in sport weight yarn is more limited than in worsted weight yarn. If you can't find sport weight yarn in the color needed, worsted weight yarn may be substituted; simply remove one ply of the yarn and stitch with the remaining three plies.

## FLOSS AND METALLICS

**Embroidery Floss** – Embroidery floss is made up of six strands. For smooth coverage when using embroidery floss, separate and realign the strands of floss before threading your needle. Twelve strands of floss may be used for covering 10 mesh canvas. Use six strands to cover 14 mesh canvas. Embroidery floss can also be used to add details on 7 mesh canvas by using six strands of floss.

**Metallic Braid or Cord** – Metallic braid or cord is available in a variety of sizes and may be used to add finishing details to a project or for general coverage. Using 18" or shorter lengths of metallic braid or cord will make stitching easier and avoid excessive wear.

**Metallic Yarn or Ribbon** – This flat yarn or ribbon is soft, flexible, and durable. Metallic yarn or ribbon can be used to add decorative details to a project or for general coverage. It is available in different sizes for use with various mesh sizes. Use 18" or shorter lengths of metallic yarn or ribbon for easier stitching and to avoid fraying. Since metallic yarn or ribbon is flat instead of round like other yarns and metallic braids, care must be used to make sure the yarn or ribbon lies flat when stitched on the canvas.

## WORKING WITH PLASTIC CANVAS

Throughout this book, the lines of the canvas will be referred to as threads. To cut plastic canvas pieces accurately, count **threads** (not **holes**) as shown in **Fig. 1**.

**Fig. 1**

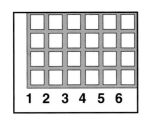

## PREPARING AND CUTTING CANVAS

Before cutting out your pieces, note the thread count located near the chart for each piece. The thread count tells you the number of threads in the width and the height of the canvas piece. It can be helpful to follow the thread count to cut out a rectangle the specified size before cutting out your shape. Then, remembering to count threads, not holes, follow the chart to trim the rectangle into the desired shape.

You may want to use an overhead projector pen to outline the piece on the canvas before cutting it out. Before you begin stitching, be sure to remove all markings with a damp towel. Any markings could rub off on the yarn as you stitch.

If there is room around your chart, it may be helpful to use a ruler and pencil to extend the grid lines of the chart to form a rectangle (see Sample Chart).

### Sample Chart

**Chicken (18 x 18 threads)**

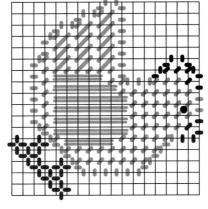

A good pair of household scissors is recommended for cutting plastic canvas. However, a craft knife is helpful when cutting out small areas. When using a craft knife, protect the table below your canvas with a layer of cardboard or a magazine.

When cutting canvas, cut as close to the thread as possible without cutting into the thread. If you don't cut close enough, "nubs" or "pickets" will be left on the edge of your canvas. Make sure to cut all nubs from the canvas before you begin to stitch, because nubs will snag the yarn and are difficult to cover.

When cutting plastic canvas along a diagonal, cut through the center of each intersection **(Fig. 2)**. This will leave enough plastic canvas on both sides of the cut so that both pieces of canvas may be used. Diagonal corners will also snag yarn less and be easier to cover.

**Fig. 2**

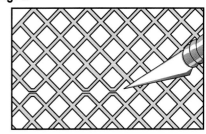

## THREADING YOUR NEEDLE

Several brands of yarn-size needle threaders are available at your local craft store. Here are a couple of methods that will make threading your needle easier without a purchased threader.

### FOLD METHOD

First, sharply fold the end of yarn over your needle; then remove needle. Keeping the fold sharp, push the needle onto the yarn **(Fig. 3)**.

**Fig. 3**

## THREAD METHOD

Fold a 5" piece of sewing thread in half, forming a loop. Insert loop of thread through the eye of your needle (Fig. 4). Insert yarn through the loop and pull the thread back through your needle, pulling yarn through at the same time.

**Fig. 4**

## READING THE CHART

Whenever possible the drawing on the chart looks like the completed stitch. For example, a tent stitch on the chart is drawn diagonally across one intersection of threads just like a tent stitch looks when stitched on your canvas. A symbol will be used on the chart when a stitch, such as a French knot, cannot be clearly drawn. If you have difficulty determining how a particular stitch should be worked, refer to the list of stitches in the project information and the Stitch Diagrams on pages 94-96.

## READING THE COLOR KEY

A color key is given with each project or group of projects. The key indicates the color used for each stitch on the chart. For example, when white yarn is represented by a grey line in the color key, all grey stitches on the chart should be stitched using white yarn.

To help you select colors for your projects, we have included color numbers for Needloft Plastic Canvas Yarn (NL) in some of our color keys. Many other different brands are available and may be used to stitch your project.

Additional information may also be included in the color key, such as the number of strands or plies to use when working a particular stitch.

## STITCHING THE DESIGN

**Securing the First Stitch** - Don't knot the end of your yarn before you begin stitching. Instead, begin each length of yarn by coming up from the wrong side of the canvas and leaving a 1" - 2" tail on the wrong side. Hold this tail against the canvas and work the first few stitches over the tail. When secure, clip the tail close to your stitched piece. Clipping the tail closely is important because long tails can become tangled in future stitches or show through to the right side of the canvas.

**Using Even Tension** - Keep your stitching tension consistent, with each stitch lying flat and even on the canvas. Pulling or yanking the yarn causes the tension to be too tight, and you will be able to see through your project. Loose tension is caused by not pulling the yarn firmly enough; consequently, the yarn will not lie flat on the canvas.

**Ending Your Stitches** - After you've completed all of the stitches of one color in an area, end your stitching by running your needle under several stitches on the back of the stitched piece. To keep the tails of the yarn from showing through or becoming tangled in future stitches, trim the end of the yarn close to the stitched piece.

## JOINING PIECES

**Straight Edges** - The most common method of assembling stitched pieces is joining two or more pieces of canvas along a straight edge using overcast stitches. Place one piece on top of the other with right or wrong sides together. Make sure the edges being joined are even, then stitch the pieces together through all layers.

**Tacking** - To tack pieces, run your needle under the backs of some stitches on one stitched piece to secure the yarn. Then run your needle through the canvas or under the stitches on the piece to be tacked in place. The idea is to securely attach your pieces without your tacking stitches showing.

**Shaded Areas** - The shaded area is part of a chart that has colored shading on top of it. Shaded areas usually mean that all the stitches in that area are used to join pieces of canvas. Do not work the stitches in a shaded area until your project instructions say you should.

**Uneven Edges** - Sometimes you'll have to join a diagonal edge to a straight edge. The holes of the two pieces will not line up exactly. Just keep the pieces even and work overcast stitches through holes as many times as necessary to completely cover the canvas.

## STITCH DIAGRAMS

> Unless otherwise indicated, bring threaded needle up at **1** and all **odd** numbers and down at **2** and all **even** numbers.

## ALICIA LACE STITCH

This series of stitches consists of simple rows of tent and reversed tent stitches (Fig. 5).

**Fig. 5**

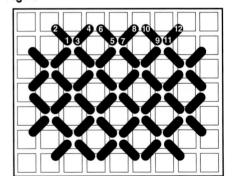

## BACKSTITCH

This stitch is worked over completed stitches to outline or define **(Fig. 6)**. It is sometimes worked over more than one thread. Backstitch may also be used to cover canvas as shown in **Fig. 7**.

**Fig. 6**

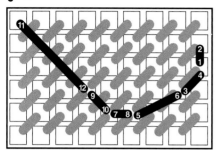

**Fig. 7**

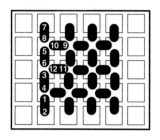

## CROSS STITCH

This stitch is composed of two stitches **(Fig. 8)**. The top stitch of each cross must always be made in the same direction. The number of intersections may vary according to the chart.

**Fig. 8**

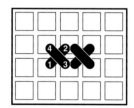

## FRENCH KNOT

Bring needle up through hole. Wrap yarn around needle once and insert needle in same or adjacent hole **(Fig. 9)**. Tighten knot as close to the canvas as possible as you pull the needle and yarn back through canvas.

**Fig. 9**

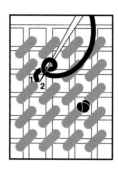

## FRINGE STITCH

Fold a length of yarn in half. Thread needle with loose ends of yarn. Bring needle up at 1, leaving a 1" loop on the back of the canvas. Bring needle around the edge of canvas and through loop **(Fig. 10)**. Pull to tighten loop **(Fig. 11)**. Trim fringe to desired length. A dot of glue on back of fringe will help keep stitch in place.

**Fig. 10**

**Fig. 11**

## GOBELIN STITCH

This basic straight stitch is worked over two or more threads or intersections. The number of threads or intersections may vary according to the chart **(Fig. 12)**.

**Fig. 12**

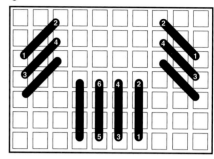

## MOSAIC STITCH

This three-stitch pattern forms small squares **(Fig. 13)**.

**Fig. 13**

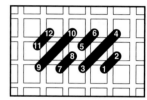

## OVERCAST STITCH

This stitch covers the edge of the canvas and joins pieces of canvas **(Fig. 14)**. It may be necessary to go through the same hole more than once to get even coverage on the edge, especially at the corners.

**Fig. 14**

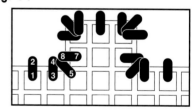

## SCOTCH STITCH

This stitch may be worked over three or more threads and forms a square. **Fig. 15** shows the Scotch stitch worked over three threads.

**Fig. 15**

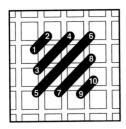

## SMYRNA CROSS STITCH

This stitch is worked over two threads as a decorative stitch. Each stitch is worked completely before going on to the next stitch **(Fig. 16)**.

**Fig. 16**

## TENT STITCH

This stitch is worked in horizontal or vertical rows over one intersection as shown in **Fig. 17**. Refer to **Fig. 18** to work the reversed tent stitch.

**Fig. 17**

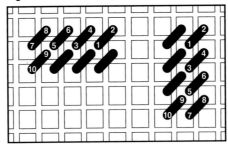

**Fig. 18**

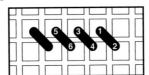

## TURKEY LOOP STITCH

This stitch is composed of locked loops. Bring needle up through hole and back down through same hole, forming a loop on top of the canvas. A locking stitch is then made across the thread directly below or to either side of the loop as shown in **Fig. 19**.

**Fig. 19**

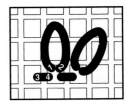

## UPRIGHT CROSS STITCH

This stitch is worked over two threads as shown in **Fig. 20**. The top stitch of each cross must always be made in the same direction.

**Fig. 20**

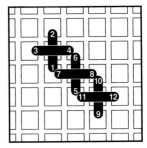

## WASHING INSTRUCTIONS

If you used washable yarn for all of your stitches, you may hand wash plastic canvas projects in warm water with a mild soap. Do not rub or scrub stitches; this will cause the yarn to fuzz. Do not dry-clean or put your stitched pieces in a clothes dryer. Allow pieces to air dry and trim any fuzz with a small pair of sharp scissors or a sweater shaver.